SOUPS and SALADS

with Schmecks Appeal

SOUPS and SALADS
with Schmecks Appeal

EDNA STAEBLER

McGraw-Hill Ryerson
Montreal   Toronto

McClelland & Stewart
Toronto

Soups and Salads with Schmecks Appeal

Copyright © 1990 Edna Staebler

First published in 1990 by

McGraw-Hill Ryerson Limited
330 Progress Avenue
Scarborough, Canada M1P 2Z5

McClelland & Stewart Publishers Ltd.
481 University Avenue
Suite 900
Toronto, Canada M5G 2E9

ISBN: 0-7710-8282-7

1 2 3 4 5 6 7 8 9 10   W   1 2 3 4 5 6 7 8 9 0

Canadian Cataloguing in Publication Data

Staebler, Edna,   - date
    Soups and salads with schmecks appeal

(Schmecks appeal cookbook series)
ISBN 0-7710-8282-7

1. Soups.   2. Salads.   3. Cookery, Mennonite.
4. Cookery - Ontario - Waterloo (Regional
municipality).   I. Title.   II. Series: Staebler,
Edna, date.   Schmecks appeal cookbook series.

TX757.S73 1990   641.8′13   C90-093712-2

Printed and bound in Canada

∞ This book was manufactured using acid-free paper.

CONTENTS

SOUPS and SALADS
with Schmecks Appeal

SOUPS

For loners and large families, couples and company, for the very young, very old, ill, or toothless, for anybody, soup is the most effective and effortless and enjoyable way to load up on vitamins.

It's so easy to make nourishing soup simply by cooking a number of vegetables — asparagus, beans, cabbage, carrots, corn, tomatoes, whatever you happen to have — fresh, frozen, or leftover. Throw in some bones, cut up an onion, cube a potato, slice a celery stick, shred a few leaves of lettuce, spinach, or cress. Add broth or salted water; season to taste with a bouquet garni, a bouillon cube, or a bay leaf. Let it simmer till you can't wait any longer. Whirl it in a blender till the mixture is smooth and anonymous. Keep tasting. Add a dollop of butter, sour cream, or wine, if you think it needs help.

Tired old casseroles smoothed in a blender with water or broth make delicious soup; so do yesterday's vegetables with giblets, poultry stuffing, and gravy. I regret not having recorded all the marvellous soups I've made out of leftovers.

You can make soup out of almost anything edible. Who's to know what's in it after it's been whirled around in a blender or pushed through a sieve? I've read recipes for soups made from an odd variety of things (although you won't find them here): peanut, she-crab, terrapin, eel ("nail eel up by the tail and peel the skin off over the head"), catfish, elderberry, calf's head ("remove the brain first"), black walnut, and cooter ("kill cooter by chopping off head"). If you want to add angostura bitters, puréed apricots, and anchovies to soup, that is your privilege. I prefer a broth with drepsly (page 31) and plenty of parsley.

You have to be daring. By guess and good luck, you'll achieve some great soups — and the odd one that even your dog wouldn't eat. I'll give you some recipes that have been approved by humans.

THE BEST VEGETABLE SOUP I'VE EVER TASTED

When Mother made this mild, thick soup with vegetables, rice, and beef, we didn't need or want anything else. The amounts I give are approximate.

    1 large, meaty beef bone
    (I think it comes from a cow's leg)
    ½ cup uncooked rice
    2 medium potatoes, sliced
    2 or 3 carrots, sliced
    1 small onion, sliced
    1 cup cut-up green beans
    1 cup cut-up celery
    ½ cup sliced cabbage
    ½ cup green peas
    Salt and pepper
    Lots of cut-up parsley

Boil the beef in water to cover till it falls off the bone. Remove the bone. You should have at least 8 cups of broth and the meat left. Add the rice and boil for 15 minutes, then add the remaining ingredients, except the parsley, and continue boiling until the vegetables are tender but not mushy — about 20 minutes. Cut the meat into more-or-less bite-sized pieces, keeping it hot in the soup. Add the parsley and serve into large, deep soup dishes — again and again.

My sister Ruby wrote me in a letter: "I'm having vegetable soup for dinner and it takes so long to peel the stuff. I'll put it through the grinder — saves time and tastes just as good — but wouldn't Mother think that was terrible? Not how she made it."

I agree with Mother. I like to see the carrot slices and pieces of celery and potato. But I do agree about the peeling; they say it's more nutritious not to peel, and scrubbing vegetables is a lot easier than taking off the skins.

A WHOLE MEAL

Soup in our family was the whole meal: it was always so rich, thick, and delicious that one dishful was just a starter. We kept passing our plates back for more and more, till the soup was all gone and our appetites, too — except for dessert.

NOODLES

Noodles are a staple in our part of the world: my Old Order Mennonite friend Bevvy and I would no more think of being without noodles in the house than we would be without potatoes or salt. They are useful for casseroles, soups, luncheon, and supper dishes; fried in butter with chicken, wiener schnitzel, and ham; or just so. Bevvy makes hers and stores them in jars; I buy mine in packages at the store, although they're not nearly as good as the egg-yellow, thicker, slightly chewy, much more flavourful noodles that Mother made fresh every time.

2 cups flour
Salt
2 eggs, or several egg yolks

Mother never measured the ingredients for noodles. Whenever she had a supply of egg yolks she wanted to use up, she'd put some flour into a bowl, slip the egg yolks into a well in the centre, and work them into the flour with a spoon till she had a smooth, stiff, yellow, pliable dough — like pie dough. Then she would divide the dough into several parts and shape each part into a ball the size of an apple. On a floured board, with a rolling pin, she would roll each ball as thin as she possibly could without tearing the dough.

The noodle dough then had to be dried. In winter she would put the rounds on a board on top of the kitchen radiator; in summer she would hang the dough over a broomstick supported by two chair backs in our sunny dining-room bay window. She would turn the pieces of dough several times during the drying. When they were dry, but not stiff, she'd put the rounds on top of each other on a board, roll them together like a jelly roll, then with a large, sharp knife, slice across the roll to make fine strips. She'd unwind the strips by tossing them lightly with her fingers, then let them keep drying on the board until she was ready to boil them in broth or salt water. If she made more than she wanted to use at the time, she'd let them dry thoroughly till they were stiff and store them away in a tightly covered jar.

BEEF NOODLE SOUP

On our birthdays Mother would cook whatever we especially wanted. I had a number of favourites but most often ordered beef noodle soup.

Fairly early in the morning, as soon as the butcher's boy delivered the meat — 3 or 4 pounds of beef with a bone full of marrow — Mother would start it boiling in a kettle of salted water. Then she would make the noodles.

About fifteen minutes before she expected us to come running down the hill from school she'd let the long, thick, egg-yellow noodles slide through her fingers into the boiling broth and cook them till they were tender.

When our hands were washed clean, our pinneys tied under our chins, and we were sitting round the big square kitchen table, she'd fish the meat out of the kettle onto a platter, stir lots of cut-up parsley into the soup, and ladle it into a tureen that she set in front of her place at the table. While we children watched and waited, Daddy cut the meat into chunks, then into bite-sized pieces on our large flat-bottomed soup plates; Mother ladled the soup on top and the birthday girl got the first serving. We blew on the hot spoonfuls and slurped up the long, lovely noodles — till Mother told us to eat like ladies. In no time our plates were empty, and we passed them back for more.

CHICKEN NOODLE SOUP

When Mother cooked a nice, old, fat **hen** for our Sunday dinner, she'd make noodle soup the next day with the **broth**, her own homemade **noodles**, and plenty of **parsley.**

NOODLE SOUP — THE HUTTERITE WAY

A long time ago, while writing a story for *Maclean's* magazine, I stayed on a Hutterite Colony in Alberta. Every morning a bell would ring to summon a group of the women to the kitchen to prepare dinner for the two hundred people living in the commune. Wearing traditional kerchiefs over their prayer caps and plaid aprons over their identically styled long dresses, the women would come with their rolling pins to make noodles several times a week.

Each woman would make her own dough, which she would then roll out as thin as parchment. She'd drape a clean dishtowel over her arm, carefully put several sheets of noodle dough over it and take them home to spread out on her bed. She'd turn them occasionally till they were dry but not stiff, roll them like a jelly roll, then return them to the kitchen to be cut in narrow slices that unrolled into noodles to be boiled in beef or chicken broth with plenty of parsley.

I visited the Hutterites again recently: the women were still being summoned by a bell to the kitchen, still wearing the traditional garb of their Bavarian ancestors. But the first thing they showed me — with great pride — was how they are now making their noodles with a noodle machine.

STOCK FOR SOUP

Our family always disdained boiling the bones of chickens or turkeys for soup stock; the idea of taking bones off people's dinner plates and putting them together into a pot somehow just didn't appeal to us. "It must be unsanitary," Mother said.

But whenever I visited the Bertons at Kleinberg, Janet, who is one of the best cooks in the world, served delicious, stylish soups made with stocks she had ladled from a huge kettle that was constantly simmering on the back of the stove. All the bones, vegetables, salad bits, and meat scraps of her household went into the pot. "The kids call it garbage soup," Janet told me, "but it's all sterilized in the cooking."

Having tried Janet's method and become a convert, I regret the mountains of bones I've wasted over the years. So many great soup recipes nonchalantly list cupfuls of stock among their ingredients: cooking bones is such an easy, economical way to keep it on hand.

When the plates come back to the kitchen, simply collect all the bones and pieces of skin that have been discarded: remove and refrigerate all the meat from the carcass, put those bones with the rest into a good-sized pot with enough boiling, salted water to cover them, then let them simmer for hours and hours, humidifying your house in the process.

Eventually pour the whole thing through a colander to strain out the bones and bits — but keep them. Cool the stock, and when the fat has congealed on top remove it for cooking and baking. Store the jelled broth in your fridge for a while, or freeze it.

More. After the first simmering of the bones, you can put them back in the kettle with water to cover and simmer them again. By this time you might have more lefovers to add, if not put in a couple of carrots, a cut-up onion, herbs or a bay leaf, some celery leaves and coarse stalks, lettuce leaves and anything else you have that might add flavour and nourishment — except starchy vegetables that disintegrate. Again let it simmer for ages. Drain it and you'll have more stock to make super soups.

A CONFESSION

I must admit that I don't always have soup stock in my freezer or fridge made from cooked bones or fat hens, ham bones or beef legs. Because so many soups require meat stock, I keep jars of chicken and beef powder that I buy at the supermarket. I also use bouillon cubes and canned broth. It's not as good as the real thing, and it has additives, which I hope won't hurt me, but it does add flavour. I've learned recently that even the purists and food columnists sometimes cheat this way — as I do.

LEEK AND POTATO SOUP

This velvety smooth soup is a cinch if you have a food processer; if you don't have one, skip it — or go out and buy one.

> **5 or 6 leeks, the white part only**
> **2 tablespoons butter**
> **3 or 4 medium potatoes**
> **3 cups chicken broth**
> **1 or 2 cups milk or cream**
> **Salt and pepper**
> **Chives or parsley**

Mince the leeks and sauté them in the butter for 3 or 4 minutes; peel and slice the potatoes very thinly, then add to the leeks along with the chicken broth. Simmer the whole bit, covered, for about 15 minutes or until all concerned are very soft. Put several ladlefuls into your food processer and twirl until it is smooth as cream. Keep on till all has been processed. Return to the pot, reheat with the addition of milk or cream — but don't let it boil. Serve very hot or very cold, garnished with chives or parsley.

CELERY SOUP PLUS

The leaves and coarse bits of celery make this soup economical and satisfying.

> **1 cup cut up celery**
> **1 cup sliced potatoes**
> **1 onion, sliced**
> **3 tablespoons flour**
> **3 cups milk**
> **3 tablespoons butter**
> **Salt and pepper**

Cook until soft the celery, potatoes, and onion in just enough water to cover them. Blend the flour into the milk and add to vegetables. Cook the mixture, stirring constantly, till it has thickened. Melt the butter on top and season. You can add chopped hard-boiled eggs to this too if you like a chowder.

CALCULATING AMOUNTS

I always hesitate to say how many people a recipe will serve. How do I know if the eaters are husky joggers, growing teenagers, or finicky slimmers? Your guess is better than mine, because you know who you are going to feed.

If you double or halve a recipe, always write the half or double amounts beside the printed figures and be sure to stick to the right column. I've ruined so many things by putting in a full amount of something when all the rest was halved.

Look over the list of ingredients, calculate roughly how many cups it all adds up to, and then double the recipe if you think you need to, or cut it in half, always remembering that it's hard to split an egg. You can freeze what's left over or eat it the next day. Some recipes can't be doubled or split without disastrous results.

The only letter I received that complained about a recipe in *Food That Really Schmecks* came from a woman who had made candy for her kids using maple syrup. The sticky, bubbling mixture boiled over and she had to clean it up; the candy didn't turn out right and her kids were disappointed. Also, maple syrup is expensive. I wrote to tell her I was sorry. She soon wrote back to apologize for her first letter and to say she had doubled the recipe and that was no doubt why it went wrong.

GLORIA DIRK'S BORSCHT

There seem to be as many ways of making borscht as there are Russian Mennonites and Ukrainians in our community who make it. Rich and flavourful, it is a complete meal.

A nice piece of beef with a bone
Several potatoes, diced
2 or 3 carrots, sliced
1 large onion, sliced (optional)
1 or 2 stalks of celery
1 quart tomatoes
1 bay leaf
Several peppercorns
Lots of dill (optional)
Several cupfuls of shredded cabbage
3 beets, cooked and chopped (optional)
Lots of parsley, cut up
Sour cream

Boil the beef in salted water until it is almost tender. Remove the bone and cut the meat into small pieces. Except the beets, parsley, and sour cream, put in all the rest of the ingredients and simmer until cooked. (Tie the dill and bay leaf together so you can fish them out.) Drop in the beets and parsley at the last minute. Put a tablespoon of sour cream on each serving and pass a bowl of cream at the table for those who want more.

GOOD AS GOLD SOUP

Don't tell anyone this soup is made with leftover cooked turnips; it is slithery-smooth, delicate, and delicious.

2 cups cooked turnip
4 cups broth (or bouillon)
Salt and pepper
1 tablespoon brown sugar
2 tablespoons butter
1 cup sweet or sour cream
1 egg or 2 yolks, beaten
Parsley or paprika

Simmer the cooked turnip in the broth for 10 minutes then rub it through a sieve or purée it in your blender till it is smooth, smooth. Heat it again as you add the other ingredients, except the egg and parsley. Stir a few tablespoons of soup into the beaten egg or yolks, remove the soup from the heat, stir the egg mixture into it till it is smooth as satin. Serve very hot with a sprinkle of parsley or paprika on top and buttered toast strips or homemade croutons alongside.

CARROT SOUP

When Cynthia Wine was the food editor of *Homemaker's* magazine she came to my house for lunch and had two helpings of this mild soup with so many of my homemade snacking crackers that I was afraid she wouldn't have space for the rest of my meal. She did!

> **1 onion, finely chopped**
> **2 or 3 tablespoons butter**
> **4 or 5 carrots, grated or finely chopped**
> **¼ cup uncooked rice**
> **6 cups beef or chicken stock**
> **Salt and pepper**
> **½ teaspoon rosemary, thyme, or mint**
> **1 or 2 teaspoons soy sauce (optional)**
> **Sour cream**

Sauté the onion in the butter until soft. Add the carrots, rice, and stock; cook gently till the rice is soft and the whole mixture has thickened. Add salt and pepper, rosemary, and soy sauce. Purée the whole bit in a blender or push it through a sieve. Reheat. It should be rich, thick, and shiny gold. Serve hot or ice-cold with a spoonful of sour cream on top. Croutons are good with this, too.

DRIED BEAN OR LENTIL SOUP

In bed at midnight when I was planning my menu for eight
people who were coming for dinner the next day, I decided to
have a cassoulet because I wasn't sure I had enough meat to go
round. I got out of bed, brought down from the top shelf of my
cupboard the box of dried beans and soaked 2 cupfuls in 2½
quarts of water. (Half limas and half brown beans with black
and white eyes. If my navy beans hadn't been so old I'd have
used them or lentils — if I'd had them.) In the morning I looked
over my supply of chicken legs, found a couple of extra ones in
my freezer, and decided I had enough to serve eight people
generously without making a cassoulet. But there were the
beans soaked and waiting to be used. Soup was the answer. And
it proved to be so popular that even the calorie-counting guests
had second helpings from the Quimper tureen I had brought
back from Brittany.

> 2 cups dried beans or lentils
> 10 cups water
> Ham bone (with or without meat)
> 2 or 3 stalks of celery, sliced
> 1 large carrot, sliced
> 1 large onion, sliced
> 1 clove garlic, chopped
> 3 tablespoons sherry (optional)
> 1½ teaspoons salt
> 1 bay leaf
> Freshly ground pepper
> Chopped parsley
> 8 slices bacon, fried crisp and
>   crumbled

Soak the beans overnight in the water (if you haven't thought
of it early enough, boil the beans in the water for a few minutes
then soak them for an hour or more). Put everything but the
parsley and bacon bits into the pot and bring to a boil, then
lower the heat and simmer the batch for about 3 hours, stirring
occasionally. Add more water if you think it needs it. Remove
bone and purée the rest in a blender or food processor or press
through a sieve — it must be smooooooooooth. Reheat. I poured
mine into my tureen and sprinkled bacon bits and parsley on
top.

CREAM OF PARSLEY SOUP

This winter I seemed to be constantly running into little pack-ages of frozen parsley in my freezer. I kept using parsley, but I knew I wouldn't be using up all those packages before I could buy fresh new parsley at the market or my sister Norm and her husband, Ralph, gave me some from their garden. I decided to splurge and to use up a whole cup-size package in one shot by making a delicate parsley soup that was as green and refreshing as the sight of Ireland.

1 cup parsley, more or less
2 cups chicken stock
3 tablespoons butter
3 tablespoons flour
2 cups milk
Pepper
½ cup fresh or sour cream
Croutons

First slice through the bunch of parsley — but not through the long tough stems; throw them away. Give the parsley and chicken broth a good whirl in your blender or food processer; then pour it into a saucepan and simmer for about 20 minutes. Meanwhile, in another saucepan, melt the butter. Blend in the flour, then the milk, stirring at medium heat until it is thick-ened. Gradually add the parsley broth and pepper. Heat it, but don't let it boil. Serve hot with a spoonful of sour cream on top. And don't forget to put a bowl of croutons on the table, or ladle the soup over a slice of bread.

If you have any surplus packages of frozen watercress or chives you might use them instead of parsley.

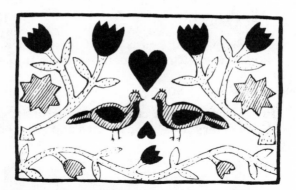

GREEN SOUP

Even non-spinach eaters will ask for a second helping of this mild cream soup. Be sure you have enough.

> **2 slices of bacon (optional)**
> **2 tablespoons bacon fat or butter**
> **1 medium onion, thinly sliced**
> **1 clove garlic, minced (optional)**
> **2 cups sliced potatoes, (raw or cooked)**
> **1½ cups boiling broth or bouillon**
> **1 cup cooked or frozen spinach —**
> **or 2 big handfuls of fresh spinach, shredded**
> **2 tablespoons butter**
> **2 tablespoons flour**
> **2 cups hot milk, or 1 cup each milk and cream**
> **Salt and pepper**

Fry the bacon till crisp, remove and drain. Leave 2 tablespoons of fat in the pan, add the onion and garlic, let sizzle gently, but do not brown. Add the potatoes and the boiling broth. Cover and let simmer till the vegetables are soft. Add the spinach and simmer 5 minutes longer. Purée in your blender, or press through a colander, and simmer again. In another saucepan, melt 2 tablespoons butter, blend in the flour, stir it till golden, add the hot milk, stir till it thickens then mix it with the vegetable purée. Serve hot with crumbled bacon on top.

CREAM OF BROCCOLI SOUP

Use **2 cups coarsely chopped cooked or raw broccoli** instead of spinach in the recipe for Green Soup. Cook the raw broccoli along with only one cup potato.

GREEN PEA SOUP

Another Green Soup — use **2 cups peas** instead of spinach and a touch of **mint or curry**. Omit the potatoes entirely, if you like.

CREAM OF CARROT SOUP

The same as Pea Soup, using **2 cups sliced carrots** and a **stalk of finely sliced celery** instead of spinach and 1 cup potatoes.

Pumpkin Soup

Use **2 cups cooked pumpkin** instead of spinach and 1 cup potato. Drop a **Bouquet Garni** into the broth.

BOUQUET GARNI

During the Stylish Entertainment course at Rundles Restaurant in Stratford, John Walker, the *chef de cuisine*, would often say, "Drop in a bouquet garni." He told us to keep a small supply on hand to use often to pep up soup, stock, or a sauce.

Cut cheesecloth or muslin into 3- or 4-inch squares and in each one put whatever herbs you like; tie up the cloth with string so the herbs can't escape, and store them in a tight jar. Don't make too many at a time; the fresher they are the better. You can vary the flavours: parsley, thyme, celery leaves, bay leaf; or parsley, chives, tarragon, chervil; or celery leaves, garlic, fennel; you might include marjoram, basil, sage, a bit of rosemary, etcetera.

NEW YEAR'S EVE OYSTER SOUP

Mother always gave us oyster soup for supper on New Year's Eve; its delicacy was achieved by making a few oysters go a long way—the price of oysters being what it was even in those days.

> **1 cup oysters**
> **4 tablespoons butter**
> **4 cups milk, heated**
> **4 or 5 soda biscuits**
> **Salt and pepper**

You may cut the oysters into pieces if you want a fairer distribution for your eaters. Melt the butter and pour the oysters with their liquor into it; stir just long enough to bring the mixture to a boil. You don't really cook the oysters at all or they'll toughen. Pour the hot milk over the oysters. Crumble the soda biscuits and stir them into the soup—using more if you like your soup thicker. Simmer the whole lot for about 2 minutes, flavour with salt and pepper, then ladle it into flat soup dishes and you're off to a Happy New Year.

WATERCRESS SOUP

A charming little French restaurant would no doubt call this delicate, delicious soup Velouté Cressonière. Some people think things taste better if they have a fancy name.

2 tablespoons butter
A large bunch of watercress
(2 or 3 cupfuls), coarsely chopped,
reserving a few perfect leaves for garnishing
6 cups boiling chicken stock
2 or 3 potatoes, peeled and sliced
Salt and pepper
2 egg yolks or 1 egg
¼ cup thick or sour cream
Lump of butter
Paprika

Melt 2 tablespoons butter in a soup kettle over medium heat. Drop in the cress and stir it around till it is somewhat limp. Add the boiling stock and the sliced potatoes. Simmer all together for about 20 minutes until the potatoes are soft. Pour the soup into a sieve and force as much as possible through it — or whirl till smooth in your blender. Bring the purée back to simmer for 2 or 3 minutes while you beat the egg yolks or egg slightly in a small bowl. Stir the cream into the egg, blending it well; stir a few spoonfuls of the hot soup into the egg mixture, take the soup off the stove and gradually stir in the egg combination. Add a lump of butter and more seasoning if you think it needs it. Heat again, but *not* to boiling point. Serve with a sprinkling of paprika on top and a few floating cress leaves.

You might substitute spinach or lettuce if watercress is hard to come by.

SPINACH SOUP

Elsie called me on a Saturday morning after a big snow in March; she said she would do some cross-country skiing ending at my place about eleven o'clock. Immediately I thought SOUP. But what kind? I had half a package of spinach that had been in my fridge long enough to become slightly limp, so I knew it must be SPINACH SOUP. (I had boiled the bones of chicken legs I'd cooked for 8 people the week before and had jellied broth waiting; I also added a tablespoon of reinforcement from my jar of chicken broth powder.)

> **Spinach –   half a package, or several handfuls, or a frozen package**
> **1 onion**
> **Water that clung to the spinach –   or ¼ cupful**
> **2 cups chicken broth**
> **2 tablespoons butter**
> **2 tablespoons flour**
> **½ cup cream or milk, or ¼ cup sour cream**

After cleaning the spinach and chopping the onion, cook them together with the water in a heavy saucepan until they are soft. Put both into a blender or food processor with 1 cupful of the chicken broth and give them a whirl until they are puréed.

Meanwhile, in the same saucepan, melt the butter over medium heat. Stir in the flour and the other cupful of broth until it is thickened. Add the spinach and onion purée. I let it almost simmer until Elsie arrived glowing and hungry. I blended in the sour cream and heated it while I put cheese croutons into a bowl on the table. Then I poured the soup into my tureen, and Elsie and I emptied it.

FROZEN TOMATOES FOR SOUPS

In late summer when tomatoes are inexpensive and beautiful, I drop at least a dozen into my freezer where they soon become hard as stones and slip into the hollow spaces as I shift things around. They look so lovely and alive and are great to discover in winter when I want to give myself a treat of tomato soup, or when I need one or two tomatoes in a recipe but not a whole can.

TOMATO CREAM SOUP

Canned tomato soups are all right when you need an instant tomato sauce to be used in a casserole or whatever, but for pure tomato soup give me the homemade variety prepared with fresh or frozen tomatoes.

> **6 fresh or frozen tomatoes**
> **1 small onion, finely chopped**
> **¼ teaspoon celery seed**
> **½ bay leaf**
> **¼ cup butter**
> **¼ cup flour**
> **3 cups milk, scalded**
> **1 teaspoon salt**
> **Pepper**
> **Parsley**

Cut the tomatoes into pieces. Put them in a saucepan with the onion, celery seed, and bay leaf; simmer uncovered for about 15 minutes, or until the tomatoes are very soft. In another pan, melt the butter. Blend in the flour, then pour in scalded milk all at once, stirring until the sauce is thick and smooth. Press the cooked tomatoes through a sieve or whirl them in a blender. Season with salt and pepper. Pour a bit at a time into the sauce, stirring vigorously. Serve with a bit of parsley sprinkled on top and with hot cheese biscuits.

TOMATO SOUP FOR ONE OR TWO

Often when I am alone, I find a tomato or two in my freezer and make this delicious cream soup.

4 tablespoons butter
3 tablespoons flour
2 cups milk or tomato juice
2 large frozen tomatoes
(or 2 cups chopped canned or raw)
Salt and pepper
2 sprigs of parsley, cut up

Melt the butter, blend in the flour; carefully add the milk and stir till the mixture thickens. Meantime, simmer the tomatoes. Strain them into the milk sauce over low heat and simmer for about 5 minutes. Season, sprinkle with parsley, and serve with or without croutons toasted and flavoured with cheese, bacon, or herbs.

LETTUCE PEA SOUP

Don't throw those rather coarse or slightly wilted lettuce leaves to the rabbits; they can be made into the kind of smooth green soup that would delight you in a ritzy restaurant.

2 cups (6 to 8 leaves) lettuce,
cut in shreds across the stem
1 small onion, minced
½ cup celery leaves (optional)
1 to 2 cups green peas
(fresh, frozen, leftover, or canned)
2 cups chicken stock
Salt and pepper
1 egg or 2 egg yolks
½ cup milk
3 tablespoons butter
1 cup cream (sweet or sour)
½ cup finely chopped parsley

Simmer the lettuce, onion, celery, and peas in the chicken stock seasoned with salt and pepper for about 15 minutes. Pour it into your blender and turn it to purée, or force it through a sieve. Beat up 2 egg yolks or a whole egg, stir in the milk, blend with the hot puréed vegetables and return to low heat, stirring till it is thickened. Just before serving, stir in the butter, cream, and half the parsley; heat it but don't let it boil. Serve with parsley sprinkled on top and croutons or buttered toast squares alongside.

MARROW BALL SOUP

Every Monday for almost twenty years Hilda Gremmelmaier came to clean my house until she died three years ago. One day she brought with her two pieces of beef leg bone and showed me how to make her favourite soup.

2 pieces of beef leg bone with marrow
8 cups salted water
1 carrot, sliced
1 celery stalk with leaves
½ onion, finely chopped
1 bay leaf
4 peppercorns
Herbs

Marrow Balls:
½ onion, chopped very finely
½ tablespoon margarine
Marrow from the bones
3 sprigs parsley, finely chopped
1 small egg
Salt and pepper
Sprinkle of nutmeg
1 to 1¼ fine dry bread crumbs

Hilda scraped all the marrow from the bones and in 2 dishes soaked bones and marrow in cold water to get rid of the redness. She kept changing the water in both until clear, breaking up the marrow with a fork and straining off the water with a sieve. She put the bones in salted water in a pot, dropped in the vegetable pieces and seasonings, and simmered them for several hours.

Meanwhile Hilda made the marrow balls. She sautéed the chopped onion in the margarine till it was soft then, with a fork, worked it into the marrow, adding the parsley, egg, seasonings, and bread crumbs until the mixture was firm enough to form into balls the size of a marble. (She tested a couple in the broth: if they came to the surface and started to disintegrate, she knew she needed more crumbs.) She placed all the little balls on a plate, covered them and put them in the fridge until eating time. She strained the broth, returned it to the pot to simmer, gently dropped all the balls into it, and turned off the heat. The moment the balls came to the surface she scooped them out and served them with the broth. If the balls are left in the pot they'd break up — but still taste good.

MARCH SOUP

Are the vegetables you've stored for the winter becoming a bit limp? Here's the way to get rid of them and enjoy the nourishment they offer. This soup is a cinch to make if you have a food processor. If you don't have one, be prepared to slice and chop all the vegetables.

The first time I went to Saint Pierre and Miquelon I stayed with Mme Dutin, who later became famous for her superb restaurant. When I was there, she served vegetable soup from a can. There was always a carafe of wine on the table, and I poured some into the soup to make it palatable. You won't have to do that with March Soup.

These amounts are approximate:

    2 onions
    3 potatoes
    2 celery stalks
    2 tomatoes (optional)
    3 carrots
    3 cups sliced cabbage
    4 to 6 cups broth, enough to cover vegetables
    2 teaspoons sugar
    Salt and pepper
    Herbs of your choice (optional)
    Sour cream
    Parsley

Finely slice or chunky-cut all the vegetables and put them into a kettle with the broth and seasonings. Cover the pot and let it simmer till all the vegetables are soft. You might need more broth. If you want your soup to be creamy, put it through the food processor and reheat it before serving with a dollop of sour cream on top and sprinkled with snipped parsley. Or serve it chunky and without the cream.

WHEATLET SPAETZLE SUPPE

Marie, a pretty, energetic strawberry blonde, has taken Hilda's place at my house; she likes to garden and to cook traditional German dishes. One morning she brought wheatlets with her so she could show me exactly how she makes her spaetzle suppe. It takes almost less time to make the soup than it does to read the directions I wrote as she made it. It needs only:

1 egg
⅓ to ½ cup wheatlets (bought in a bulk food store)
A good meat stock
Parsley or chives

Marie beat the egg lightly with a fork. Because it was a small egg, she measured ⅓ cup wheatlets and blended it with the egg. The mixture was fairly runny. She let it stand for perhaps 10 minutes and the wheatlets had swelled and become stiff enough to be like a soft porridge. Meanwhile she put the stock on to boil. Because I didn't have real chicken or beef stock, I used chicken broth mix (and I used more than the directions on the jar directed and the broth was too salty).

Marie dipped a teaspoon into the rapidly boiling broth to warm it, then she scooped about ½ teaspoon of the wheatlet mixture, and again dipped the spoon into the broth to let the mixture stay there. She kept dropping off spoonfuls until all the mixture was in the broth, which was turned down to simmer. All the neat little elliptical spaetzle were floating on top. After 10 to 15 minutes, they swelled slightly and Marie tested one to make sure they were no longer soft in the centre. (She said the broth should not be too salty or the spaetzle might be tough.)

When it was ready to serve, Marie sprinkled finely cut parsley and chives over the soup and we ate every bit, steaming hot.

This long palaver about making it may sound complicated, but it really is a very simple operation—once you get the hang of it—and a pleasant change from noodle soup. Your guests and family will be intrigued and will wonder how you made all those perfect little dumplings.

You could make them with stew or chicken potpie. Marie told me that sometimes she has a craving to cook spaetzle in milk instead of broth; she sprinkles it with sugar and cinnamon. A good mild dish to have if you're feeling a bit out-of-sorts.

PEA POD SOUP

To save juicy fresh pea pods from the compost heap, my English friend Kath devised this delicious, delicate soup that is bothersome to prepare but really special. Whenever she comes from Devon to visit, I get her to make it.

2 or 3 quarts strictly fresh pea pods
(if they're limp, throw them out)
6 tablespoons butter
1 small onion, or 1 leek, chopped
2 tablespoons flour
2 cups milk
Salt
1 tablespoon butter
½ cup cream
2 fresh mint leaves

As soon the peas are podded, Kath sweats the pods in 3 tablespoons of the butter in a heavy pan with the chopped onion. She keeps stirring them over medium heat until they are soft, then she rubs them through a sieve. (I thought I'd save a lot of trouble by putting them into my blender but the fibre of the pods was so tough it almost ruined the machine by wrapping around the blades. It has to be done the hard way.)

Kath then makes a cream sauce by stirring the flour into 2 tablespoons of melted butter and adding the milk. When it has thickened, she stirs in the pea pod purée, melts in the remaining 1 tablespoon of butter, and adds cream to make it superb. She served it hot with a bit of chopped mint leaf on top. "But don't overdo it," she warns. "The flavour of the pods is delicate and could be overpowered."

VERDIE VANDEPOL'S ASPARAGUS SOUP

A few years ago when I had pneumonia, Verdie sent me a big bowl of this wonderful soup. It saved my life. And that isn't all: every day that I was sick Verdie sent her husband, Tony, over to my house with a complete meal nicely served on a tray with a flower in a vase to cheer me. Such caring neighbours, the attention of other friends, and penicillin made me recover very quickly.

4 or 6 spears fresh asparagus, sliced thin
1 or 2 cloves garlic, minced
1 stalk celery, thinly sliced
1 green pepper, chopped
4 cups chicken stock
Salt and pepper
Crisp bits of fried bacon

Combine asparagus, garlic, celery, green pepper, and chicken stock. Bring to a boil, then simmer until the vegetables are tender, about 10 minutes. Add a pinch of salt and pepper. Serve hot, garnished with bacon bits.

KARTOFFEL SUPPE
(Potato Soup)

Minnie Vogel can't eat onions: she makes her potato soup this way. "Smoos as welvet," she told me.

2 cups potatoes, sliced
(Minnie sometimes uses leftover potatoes)
1 big carrot, thinly sliced
1 stalk celery, cut finely
6 cups chicken or beef broth
⅛ teaspoon marjoram
Salt and pepper
2 tablespoons butter
3 tablespoons flour
2 or 3 tablespoons chopped parsley

Put the potatoes, carrot, and celery into a pot with boiling stock and seasonings; boil gently until the vegetables are very tender. Put them through a colander or purée them in a blender, return to the heat and let simmer. Melt the butter, add the flour and stir until it is golden. Gradually stir in some of the soup stock, then blend with the rest of the soup. Stir and let it simmer 10 minutes longer, till it is bound together. When you serve it, add the parsley, sprinkling some on top.

Bevvy's Mennonite Soups

*The steaming soup bowl is passed around Bevvy Martin's
table at suppertime, and we ladle into our plates its clear,
fragrant broth thickened by tiny dumplings. Bevvy says,
"Grossmommy Brubacher always told me drepsly (dripped
batter) soup is especially nourishing for the sick."*

*"But I ain't sick," Bevvy's husband, David, says. His
bright brown eyes are teasing. "I guess that's why I rather
always would have bean soup."*

*"Ach, you like any thick soup where I sprinkle buttered
browned bread crumbs on," Bevvy says with a smug little
smile.*

"Except rivel soup," her little son Amsey reminds her.

*"It is made from milk thickened with eggs and flour
rubbed into rivels (crumbs)," her daughter Lyddy tells me.*

*"He eats that, too, if he has a slice of raw onion and
summer sausage with it," Bevvy says.*

*"Ach, I eat anything, if I like it real good or not. That's
how we are taught not to waste." David holds his spoon
like a sceptre.*

"Have you never tried canned soup?" I ask him.

*"We never bought a can of anything yet," Bevvy answers.
"We always chust make our own."*

*"We got more different kinds yet than they got in the
stores," daughter Salome says. "We make soup from our
vegetables, from our meat, from our leftovers, and we have
all kinds of milk soups." She pauses to sop up the remains
of her drepsly soup with buttered bread to clean her plate
for kochkase, summer sausage, and pickled beets. "I think
we make soup out of everything you could put in your
mouth to eat."*

*"Ach, Salome, that ain't right," Amsey looks at his sister
reproachfully, "You know we never yet had soup made
from huckleberry pie."*

CHICKEN AND CORN SOUP WITH RIVELS

This rich, thick, Mennonite soup is the most special there is. Bevvy says they always make it for company.

> **1 cut-up chicken; you can use pieces,**
> **but old hens have the best flavour**
> **8 cups salted water**
> **½ cup cut-up celery, stalks and leaves**
> **1 medium onion, sliced**
> **Corn cut from 6 or 8 cobs (or a can or two of**
> **niblets for deprived city dwellers)**
> **Salt and pepper**
> **2 hard-boiled eggs, chopped**
> **4 tablespoons cut-up parsley**
> **Cream**
>
> *Rivels:*
> **1 cup flour**
> **1 egg, beaten**
> **A bit of milk if necessary**

Cook the chicken in the salted water until the meat is tender and can be easily removed from the bones. Cut it into bite-sized pieces and put the meat back into the broth without cooling it any more than you have to. Add celery, onion, corn, and seasonings; boil about 15 minutes while you make the rivels by rubbing the flour and egg mixture into crumbs. Add milk if needed. Drop the rivels into the boiling soup, stirring to prevent them from becoming a single mass; cover and simmer for 7 minutes. Now add the chopped egg and the parsley. Serve from a soup tureen on the table and pass cream to be poured into the soup.

SOUPS WITH HAM BROTH

Don't ever throw away the liquid that ham was boiled in; after you've let it cool and have skimmed off the fat, it can be the perfect base for delicious soups.

HAM AND VEGETABLE SOUP

The stock, bone, and some leftover ham make this vegetable soup a complete meal.

1 pound dried navy or soup beans
4 cups ham broth
Ham bone
2 cups chopped canned or fresh tomatoes
2 onions, sliced
½ cup chopped celery leaves or stalks
2 tablespoons cut-up parsley
Leftover ham

Soak the beans overnight, drain and cook in the ham broth with the bone until tender. Add the other vegetables and cook them till they are soft. Remove the bone, add the parsley and pieces of leftover ham. Simmer for a few minutes, then serve. It will be thick and delicious.

BEVVY'S BOHNA SUPP
(Bean Soup)

This is David's favourite; Bevvy makes it often, and after having it for supper with the Martins I know why.

1 pound dried soup beans
8 cups salted water or ham broth
2 cups milk
Salt and pepper
Butter the size of half a large egg
3 slices bread, cut in cubes

Soak the beans overnight in water to more than cover them. Pour off the water and cover the beans with 8 cups salted fresh water—or ham broth—and boil them till they are tender. There should be some water left on the beans. Add the milk and seasonings and simmer till it is hot. Meanwhile brown the butter carefully, add the bread cubes and stir them around till they all get the taste of the butter and are a bit brown. Put the bread into the soup, pour the soup into a bowl and serve it piping hot.

With the soup we ate summer sausage on slices of home-baked bread. When the soup was "all," and sopped up with the bread, we put canned raspberries and kochkase on our plates and ate them with Bevvy's molasses cookies, then her Quick Pudding, hot from the oven and rich with brown sugar sauce.

DRIED PEA SOUP

Here is another of Bevvy's tasty fillers.

> **2 cups dried peas**
> **8 cups water or ham broth**
> **1 large onion, sliced**
> **3 tablespoons butter**
> **1 stalk celery, cut up**
> **1 cup sliced potatoes**
> **Salt and pepper**
> **¼ cup bread crumbs**

Soak the peas overnight in plenty of water; drain, put them in the 8 cups of water (or ham broth) and boil until tender. Brown the onion in 1 tablespoon of the butter and add to peas with the celery and potatoes. Cook slowly until they too are tender. Season with salt and pepper. Brown the breadcrumbs in remaining butter and sprinkle them over the soup when you serve it. If you have any mild leftover vegetables you may add them.

VARIATIONS: You might like to put the soup through a colander (or blender) and simmer for a moment after. Or you might add small pieces of cooked smoked pork sausage when you put in the onion, celery, and potatoes.

ONION SOUPS

Because Bevvy can keep onions in the cellar all winter, tzvivelle supp in various versions is a standby when the snow flies.

TZVIVELLE SUPP MITT KASE
(Onion Soup With Cheese on Toast)

I wonder if a Mennonite woman went out one night and had French onion soup, which she then interpreted this way for her family.

> 1½ cups chopped or sliced onions
> 2 cups boiling salted water
> 2 cups milk
> A large lump of butter
> Pepper
> 4 slices buttered toast
> 1 cup grated cheese

Cook the onions in salted water till tender, add the milk and simmer together about 10 minutes. Add butter and pepper. Put a slice of buttered toast in each flat-bottomed soup dish, heap grated cheese on the toast, pour the soup over it, and you won't waste any time eating it.

TZVIVELLE RIVEL SUPP
(Onion Rivel Soup)

Can you resist that name? It tasted good, too, at Bevvy's house.

> 4 medium onions, sliced (about 2 cups)
> 4 tablespoons butter
> 5 or 6 cups beef broth
> Salt and pepper
> Flour
> 1 beaten egg

Cook the onions in butter until lightly browned. Heat the broth, add the onions, bring to a boil, then simmer. Season with salt and pepper. For the rivels: add enough flour to the beaten egg to form crumbs. Let the rivels fall in flakes into the soup and simmer, covered, for about 10 minutes till the rivels are cooked, the soup thick.

SALSIFY OR MOCK OYSTER SOUP

Bevvy says the delicate flavour of salsify soup is just like oyster soup without the oysters.

1½ cups cut-up salsify (oyster plant)
1½ cups salted water
3 tablespoons butter
3 cups milk
Salt and pepper
Bread cubes browned in butter

Cook salsify in salted water until tender. Add butter and milk and heat to a boil. Season and serve with bread cubes.

GRAESHT MEHL GRUMBARA SUPP
(Brown Flour Potato Soup)

Bevvy calls this "real Old Mennonite soup."

6 medium potatoes
3 cups salted water
3 cups milk
3 tablespoons flour
3 tablespoons butter
Salt and pepper
Parsley

Peel and cut the potatoes in slices. Boil them in salted water until tender. Add the milk and let simmer. Meanwhile brown the flour in the melted butter, stirring all the time at low heat; add it to the soup, keep stirring till the mixture thickens. Season and sprinkle with parsley. Serve with buttered crumbs, or squares of fried bread, or pretzels on top. You might boil some sliced onion with the potatoes, if you like.

DREPSLY SUPP

This Old Mennonite favourite is easy and fun to make. "Drepsly" means little drops or dribbles. And the soup is delicious.

    1 egg
    ½ cup flour
    ¼ cup milk
    4 cups beef or chicken broth
    Lots of cut-up parsley
    Salt

Beat the egg, blend in the flour, then the milk. The batter must be runny. When the meat broth is boiling rapidly, put a colander over it and pour the batter through it into the broth, stirring to quicken the dribbling. Quickly put on the lid, turn the heat down to half, and cook slowly for four minutes in the covered kettle. Take off the lid, turn off the heat, add the parsley and salt and serve the soup immediately so the dreps — like very tiny dumplings — don't absorb too much of the broth.

RIVEL SUPP

Though this may not be David's favourite, Bevvy says it is warm and comforting if your stomach is a little queasy or if you've just had all your teeth out; it is also good for the sick and the very young.

    4 cups milk
    ½ teaspoon salt
    1 large egg
    1 cup flour

While you are heating the milk and salt in the top of a double boiler, beat the egg, add the flour and mix them with two knives, then with your hands until the mixture forms lumps the size of cherry stones. Let these rivels fall lightly into the hot milk. Keep the milk over the boiling water for five minutes, until the rivels are blended with the milk. It will be thick and nourishing.

    Rivels can be used to give body to any number of soups made with vegetables, broth, or milk.

MILK TOAST

I've never tried Bevvy's Rivel Soup for the Sick. When we weren't feeling well, Mother used to give us a slice of buttered toast with white or brown sugar and cinnamon sprinkled over it, then enough hot milk to thoroughly soak it and partly fill the soup dish. We liked it so well that we sometimes had it when we weren't sick.

SMOKED SAUSAGE SOUP

A good, gutsy, masculine Mennonite soup with that old-fashioned smoky flavour.

>   **At least ½ pound smoked pork sausage**
>   **8 cups water**
>   **2 or 3 cups sliced cabbage**
>   **½ small turnip or 4 large potatoes**
>   **2 carrots**
>   **1 stalk celery**
>   **1 onion**
>   **Salt**
>   **Milk or cream**

While the pork sausage is boiling gently in water, slice all the vegetables. Add vegetables and salt to the sausage, stir occasionally. Cook about 20 minutes until the vegetables are soft and the bree (stock) is very thick. Remove the sausage and slice to ¼-inch pieces. Return sausage to soup, pour in some milk or cream to thin the soup if you like, cover and heat. Don't bother making anything else when you serve this; it's a meal.

CANNED VEGETABLE SOUP

Eva makes this when the tomatoes are ripe in her garden. It's a lot of work. "It takes a whole day," she says, "and when you're done you're thankful. But it's so nice to have in the winter when you just have to heat it for soup or a sauce for macaroni, or with noodles and meat in a casserole. You can vary it as much as you like — put in whatever you have, leave out what you don't like."

> 1 quart carrots, cut up
> 1 quart peas
> 1 quart yellow string beans, cut in pieces
> 1 quart corn, cut from cob
> 1 quart cabbage, cut fine
> 5 onions, finely chopped
> 3 to 5 green peppers
> 1 cup navy beans, soaked overnight and boiled till soft before adding
> 1 cup barley, soaked several hours, then boiled a long time before adding
> 4 gallons of tomato juice
> ¼ cup sugar
> ¼ cup salt (but taste as you add)
> 1 to 2 cups chopped parsley

Cook each vegetable separately in boiling water for about 10 minutes — the beans and barley longer. Combine all the cooked vegetables and tomato juice in a huge kettle. Add the sugar and salt and more tomato juice if you think the mixture is too thick. Boil 10 minutes longer. Stir in parsley. Seal in sterilized jars and steam the small jars for 10 minutes. Eva says she steams hers 20 to be sure and 30 minutes for the quart jars. She adds more tomato juice when she heats it for serving as soup.

Cold Soups

Chilled soup and a salad is a perfect company lunch for a hot day in summer. The soup can be prepared in the early cool of the morning—or a day or two before your guests are expected.

CHILLED CUCUMBER SOUP

This is an easy way to make chilled cucumber soup—and so refreshing.

> **3 cucumbers**
> **¼ cup butter**
> **1 leek, sliced**
> **1 bay leaf**
> **1 tablespoon flour**
> **3 cups chicken stock**
> **Salt**
> **1 cup cream**
> **1 teaspoon finely chopped dill or mint**
> **Pepper**
> **Sour cream**

Peel and thinly slice the cucumbers. Sauté in butter with leek and bay leaf until tender but not brown. Stir in the flour; add the chicken stock and salt. Simmer, covered, for 30 minutes; remove the bay leaf. Cool. Press through a sieve or purée in a blender. Stir in cream, dill, and pepper. Chill in fridge for at least 30 minutes. Serve in soup bowls with a fluff of sour cream on top.

CUCUMBER VICHYSSOISE

A refreshing first cousin of vichyssoise: nourishing cold soup to serve on a hot summer day. It can be made a day or two ahead and kept in your fridge.

> 1 medium onion, or 1 leek,
>   or green onions with leaves, sliced
> 2 tablespoons butter
> 1 unpeeled cucumber, diced
> 1 large potato, sliced (or 1 cup leftover or
>   mashed potato)
> 2 cups chicken broth or bouillon
> Several sprigs parsley
> ½ teaspoon thyme
> Salt and pepper
> 1 cup thick or sour cream
> Chopped chives

Cook the onion in butter until it is transparent but not brown. Add the remaining ingredients, except the cream and chives; bring to a boil. Lower the heat and simmer until the potatoes are tender, about 25 minutes. Purée in your blender or put the mixture through a colander. (I blend mine then put it through a sieve to remove the cucumber seeds.) Taste for seasonings. There's nothing to prevent you from eating this soup hot, but it's best when chilled thoroughly. Before serving, stir in the cream, sprinkle the chives on top. I serve it with hot cheese biscuits or cheese onion squares.

CHILLED BEET SOUP

Instead of a cucumber, use **1 cup sliced, cooked beets**, but don't put them into the soup till you are ready to put the mixture into your blender.

COLD TOMATO SOUP

Whirled in a blender this is quick, easy, and tasty.

> **3 or 4 cups unpeeled tomatoes (fresh,**
>   **frozen, or canned)**
> **¼ cup chopped green onions or**
>   **1 regular onion, chopped**
> **2 teaspoons cornstarch**
> **1 tablespoon lemon juice**
> **Pinch of powdered thyme**
> **1 teaspoon salt**
> **1½ teaspoons sugar**
> **Pepper**
> **½ to 1 cup sour cream**
> **Chopped parsley**

Drop all ingredients but sour cream and parsley into the blender and whirl till perfectly smooth. Put through a sieve to remove tomato seeds. Bring to a slow boil until thickened. Before serving, hot or chilled, stir in sour cream and sprinkle parsley on top.

CHILLED AVOCADO SOUP

Buy ripe avocados and in minutes you can make this beautiful soup, rich in vitamin C.

> **1 or 2 avocados**
> **1 cup chicken broth (or chicken concentrate**
>   **dissolved in hot water and chilled)**
> **½ cup milk**
> **1 teaspoon minced onion or shallot**
> **Salt and pepper**
> **Croutons**

Scrape enough avocado from the shell to make 1 cup or so. Put all the ingredients in your blender or processor and keep it whirling until the mixture is smoooooooooooth. (Mash the avocado if you don't have a blender or food processor.) Pour into a covered container and put it in your fridge until chilled. Serve with crisp herb-flavoured croutons. You won't need much more for a meal.

If you are lucky enough to be able to buy a number of avocados from the mark-down table at the supermarket, double or triple the recipe and have a party.

ALMOND SOUP

This is for a special treat. Easy to make and can be served hot or cold.

> ½ **cup blanched almonds**
> 3 **cups milk**
> 1 **teaspoon minced onion or shallot**
> ½ **stalk celery, chopped**
> 1 **tablespoon butter**
> 2 **teaspoons flour**
> **Cayenne pepper**
> **Salt**
> ¼ **cup toasted almond slivers**

Put the almonds through the fine blade of a food grinder. Simmer in 1 cup of the milk with onion and celery. Blend butter and flour and add remaining 2 cups of milk gradually. Stir into almond mixture and cook, stirring all the time, until it reaches the thickness of cream soup. Season with a pinch of cayenne and salt. Top each serving with toasted almond slivers.

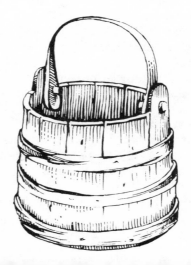

CHILLED CHERRY SOUP

In beautiful Berne, Switzerland, a friend sometimes took me to delightful vegetarian restaurants in which they started a meal with chilled fruit soup. This will surprise and delight your friends on a day in summer.

> 1 pound sour cherries
> 3 cups water
> 2 tablespoons sugar (or more)
> Zest of 1 lemon
> 1 tablespoon cornstarch

Wash and pit the cherries, then put them in a saucepan with the water, sugar, and thinly peeled lemon rind. Simmer gently. Rub through a sieve or purée in a blender. Blend cornstarch in a tablespoon of cold water. Gradually stir in the purée and simmer again for 5 minutes, stirring all the time until thickened and translucent. Serve icy cold.

Try this with strawberries or raspberries too—or have it for dessert.

RHUBARB MUS (SOUP)

The Russian Mennonites serve this soup hot or cold. I prefer it chilled as a dessert, with cookies that are not too sweet. It is really good.

> 4 cups sliced rhubarb
> 4 cups water
> 1 cup raisins (optional)
> 1 cup sugar
> 2 tablespoons flour or cornstarch
> 1 cup cream

Cook the rhubarb, water, and raisins until tender, then add the sugar mixed with the flour, stirring until the mixture is thickened. Stir in the cream and serve hot or cold. Stirring it with a cinnamon stick gives it a piquant flavour.

PRUNE MOOS

A popular European soup that can be eaten hot or chilled "at the front or back part of a meal," a Mennonite friend told me.

2 cups prunes
1 cup raisins
½ cup sugar
1 teaspoon cinnamon (optional)
3 tablespoons flour or 2 tablespoons cornstarch
½ teaspoon salt
1 cup cream

Cover the prunes and raisins with water and cook until tender; remove the fruit. Combine the sugar, cinnamon, flour, and salt; blend together with enough water to make a thick pouring consistency and stir into the water in which the fruit was cooked; stir over low heat until thick as white sauce. Add the fruit. Stir in the cream and heat but don't boil.

Moos or Mus is sometimes made with buttermilk instead of water. It is also made with a variety of fruits, dried, raw, or canned: cherries, plums, rhubarb, apples, gooseberries, apricots. It can be made in advance and reheated, or chilled and used as a dessert.

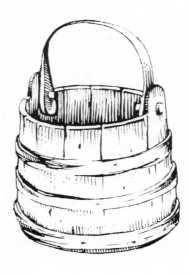

SALADS

*Bevvy has never bought oil for a salad and Mother
despised it as something fit only for axles. Sour cream with
a bit of salt, pepper, sugar, and vinegar is the favoured
dressing for most Waterloo County salads. It is poured over
tender leaf lettuce or spinach leaves, thinly sliced
cucumbers, dandelion greens, boiled schnippled
(Frenched) string beans, chopped cabbage, endive, onions,
and potatoes; sometimes it is thickened and warm,
sometimes it is chilled; always it is rich and surprisingly
zestful.*

*A sour-cream salad is never a basic meal — as it might
be for a modern luncheon; it is never a separate course; it
is something delightfully subtle and fresh to be eaten as a
vegetable with an entrée. Garnished with hard-boiled eggs
and bacon bits; served with smoked pork chops or
sausages, roasted pigs' tails, or spare ribs with a schnitz
pie for dessert, you'll have a memorable meal.*

*Ever since I learned that sour cream has 50 calories per
tablespoon and salad oil has 125, I have enjoyed with a
clear conscience the kinds of salads my mother used to
make.*

*Bevvy has no recipes for salads in her little hand-written
cookbook, and in Mother's there are recipes only for those
she made when she entertained friends and her bridge
club. They never measured exactly what they put into a
salad. They made experienced guesses about the amounts
of vegetables and greens they might need for the number of
people they were feeding, and they kept schmecking
(tasting) the sour-cream dressing till it seemed to be just
about right.*

*The amounts I've specified in the recipes here are as
accurate as I can make them after frequent and impatient
measuring with teaspoons and cups. A sour-cream salad
should be rich, buttery, and delicate — not sour; I use
cider or red wine vinegar, which I think is less strident,
and very little of either; Mother would have used even less,
and Bevvy puts in more sugar.*

*Since flavouring the dressing is a personal thing, I'm
afraid you'll just have to consider my recipes as a guide*

*from which to develop a formula that tastes right to you,
that will give you and yours the same lip-smacking
pleasure that sour-cream salads have been giving to the
natives of Waterloo County since the first cow was led up
here through forest and swamp land from far-away
Pennsylvania in 1798.*

*Besides sour-cream salads I have tried to give you
variety: accompanying salads, salads that are a whole
meal, crisp salads that will keep for a week in your fridge,
and a few salad dressings.*

YOGURT INSTEAD FOR SOUR CREAM SALADS

*If you are a martyr, you can use yogurt instead of sour
cream in all of Bevvy's recipes. It has fewer calories, less
body, and less flavour. Bevvy and Mother and I would
never try it. Substitutes are just substitutes.*

LETTUCE SALAD

When Waterloo Country gardens are flourishing, a lettuce salad
appears on dinner tables every day. Tender, soft, yellow butter
lettuce, red speckled, oak leaf, and vivid green leaf-lettuce are
the favourite varieties; the solid, crisp head lettuce that is
imported and sold in the supermarkets is seldom used with this
sour-cream dressing.

**Enough lettuce leaves for 4 people
About ½ cup sour cream
1 teaspoon sugar
1 teaspoon vinegar
Fresh chives, finely cut, or finely sliced onions
Salt and pepper
1 hard-boiled egg (optional)**

Wash and dry the lettuce. Stir the other ingredients together
and pour over the lettuce, mix lightly. A sliced hard-boiled egg
may be used as a garnish if you want to be fancy or give it more
body. This salad won't keep long — it should be served immediately or the lettuce will wilt and be miserable.

SCHNIPPLED BEAN SALAD
(Frenched Bean Salad)

Whenever the Berton family comes to visit me, I make bean salad because it is Pierre's favourite; he always watches me mix it, sticks a finger into the sour-cream dressing, licks it off, and says, "Great!"

This most popular Waterloo County specialty serves as both salad and vegetable. How many beans to use is a problem: people always eat more than they think they can; one summer Sunday when I had ten guests for dinner, I used six quarts of fresh yellow beans for the salad and there was just a nappieful left.

> **1 quart green or yellow string beans**
> **1 smallish onion**
> **Salt**
>
> *Dressing:*
> **1 teaspoon sugar**
> **1 teaspoon vinegar**
> **½ teaspoon salt**
> **Pepper**
> **¾ cup sour cream**

Cut the stems off the beans, wash them, then schnipple them — that means cutting the beans on a slant in very thin slices, one bean being cut into 3 or 4 long slices. (Or you could use frozen Frenched beans.) Put the beans into boiling salted water and cook them just long enough to be barely soft. Drain and cool them. Meantime, peel and slice the onion and sprinkle it liberally with salt and stir it around; let it stand at least 15 minutes, giving it a stir now and then.

In a bowl large enough to contain the beans, put the sugar, vinegar, ½ teaspoon salt, a good sprinkling of pepper, and sour cream. Stir all together. Now take the salted onion into your hand and with the other hand squeeze as much of the juice out of it as you can. Put the squeezed onion into the dressing, pour the drained beans into the bowl and mix with the dressing till all the beans are generously coated — you might need more cream.

Some people like the beans to be slightly warm or hot — but then the dressing becomes thin and runny and doesn't properly coat the beans. Some like the squeezed juice of the onion in the dressing as well as the onions. Some like more onions. If by some strange miscalculation the bean salad isn't all eaten, you can put it in your fridge and keep it for a day or two.

CUCUMBER SALAD

Cool, fresh, and delicious on a hot summer day with cold meat left over from Sunday and tiny boiled new potatoes browned in butter and sprinkled with parsley. But just as good in winter with a piping hot dinner. Cucumber salad gives a piquant touch to any meal.

2 large cucumbers
Salt
1 small onion (or chives)

Dressing:
½ cup sour cream
1 teaspoon sugar
1 teaspoon vinegar (or less)
Pepper

Peel the cucumber and slice it thinly. Sprinkle it with salt and slosh it around a bit so the salt is well distributed among all the slices. Now peel the onion and slice it finely, too; sprinkle it with salt. Let both cucumber and onion stand in their separate dishes for about 15 minutes, giving each a swish whenever you happen to pass. Squeeze the onion between your fingers, using both hands and leaving the slices quite limp. In the same way, squeeze the juice from the cucumbers — only don't squeeze quite so hard.

Combine the onion and cucumber and over them pour and stir a dressing made of the sour cream, sugar, vinegar, and pepper.

And that's it. If there's any left it will keep in the fridge to be eaten next day; Mother loved to finish it up with her breakfast.

TZVIVELLE SALAT

A lot of people around here are crazy about this.

2 large Spanish onions or 3 Italian onions
Salt

Dressing:
½ cup thick sour cream
1 teaspoon sugar
1 teaspoon wine vinegar
Pepper

Slice the onions very thin, separate the rings and sprinkle all lightly with salt; let stand for about 15 minutes; then over them pour and stir a dressing made of the sour cream, sugar, vinegar, and pepper.

EVA'S BROCCOLI SALAD

Eva makes this for company and she says no one ever leaves her house without taking a copy of this recipe. It's a really good one.

1 bunch broccoli,
flowerets and stems chopped fairly fine
At least ½ mild red or Spanish onion,
sliced and chopped
8 slices bacon, fried crisp and crumbled

Dressing:
½ cup mayonnaise
½ cup sour cream
2 tablespoons vinegar
⅓ cup sugar

Combine the broccoli, onion, and bacon. Mix the dressing ingredients, pour them over broccoli mixture, mix well and let stand for an hour before serving. There won't be any left over.

COLESLAW

Not at all like the wretched sour stuff you get in most restaurants.

    4 cups chopped cabbage
    1 small onion, chopped
    ½ cup thick sour cream
    2 teaspoons sugar
    1 teaspoon vinegar
    Salt and pepper

Combine cabbage and onion. Mix the other ingredients together, pour the mixture over the cabbage and onion and combine them. If you want more nip, add a pinch of mustard or a teaspoon of horseradish.

    This salad goes quite a long way and is best eaten with a dinner.

WALPER HOTEL SPINAT SALAT
(Spinach Salad)

Dozens of diners at Kitchener's Walper Hotel tried to figure out exactly how this super salad was made. Joe Zuber, the owner of the hotel, gave the recipe to me.

    1 pound spinach
    ¼ cup crumbled, crisply fried bacon

Dressing:
    1 cup table cream
    3 tablespoons white vinegar
    1 teaspoon grated onion
    1 teaspoon prepared mustard
    Salt, pepper, and sugar

Wash the spinach well in several changes of clear cold water. Cut away the tough stems and discard them. Drain the spinach leaves and chill in a damp cloth. Roll a handful of leaves and slice with a very sharp knife into quarter-inch strips. Combine dressing ingredients. Toss the spinach with the dressing and serve on a bed of leaf lettuce; sprinkle the crumbled fried bacon on top.

MOTHER'S GREEN LEAF SALAD

Mother often gave us this wonderful salad that seemed to be just right with whatever else she served. Sometimes she used only spinach leaves, or endive, or a mixture of both with some lettuce.

> **As many greens as you need for
>   the number of people you're serving**
> **1 slice of bacon per person to be served,
>   cut in ¼-inch pieces**
> **1 teaspoon brown sugar**
> **Salt and pepper**
> **½ teaspoon mild vinegar per serving**
> **3 tablespoons sour cream per serving, or less**
> **½ hard-boiled egg per person, sliced or chopped**

Wash and drain the greens and remove coarse stems. Fry the bacon bits till crisp, remove and drain. To the bacon fat in the pan over low heat, add the sugar and stir till it's more or less melted; stir in the salt and pepper and gently add the vinegar, being careful lest it spit. (The sugar might become hard. If so, let it melt.) Blend well and let cool before you blend in the sour cream. It should be smooth and the thickness of mayonnaise; you might need more cream. Just before serving, pour it over the mixed greens torn to bite-sized pieces. Toss gently to get some of the sauce on all the greens: not soggy — just nicely coated, but not skimpy either. . . . Add more cream if you haven't enough. Garnish with the bacon bits and hard-boiled eggs.

The oftener you make this, the more adept you will become at judging the amounts for the dressing. It's really quite simple, unusual, and the best tossed salad I know.

I might add that as you keep multiplying the amount of the ingredients by the number of people you are going to be serving, you might want to pour off some of the bacon fat and reduce the amounts of sugar and vinegar.

CANNED TOMATO SALAD

For supper one night at Bevvy's, I found this salad surprisingly good and refreshing — with fried potatoes and summer sausage and kochkase.

> **2 cups drained, canned tomatoes cut in quarters**
> **2 or 3 hard-boiled eggs, sliced or chopped coarsely**
> **2 teaspoons mayonnaise**
> **Salt and pepper**

Stir all together and it's ready to serve.

DADDY'S TOMATOES

My father liked his tomatoes sliced into a nappy with brown sugar, salt, pepper, and vinegar sprinkled over them. Mother was scornful but one day consented to taste the concoction: she became a convert — using white sugar instead of brown.

Warm Salads

Any Mennonite woman will tell you to use a warm sour-cream dressing for endive, spinach, cabbage, potatoes, or dandelion greens. Garnished with hard-boiled eggs and bacon bits, served with cold meats or sausages, you'll need nothing more to make a meal. Except, perhaps, shoo-fly pie.

DANDELION SALAD

Any old-timer in Waterloo County will tell you that dandelion greens will purify your blood, grown sluggish and thick through the winter. As soon as spring comes, I have a compulsive hunger for dandelion salad. I could — and should — dig the dandelions out of my lawn the moment they appear, young and tender; but I lazily buy the long, bleached stems with yellow-green leaves that some Mennonite farmers cultivate under sawdust or straw and sell at the Kitchener market — though they say the natural green dandelion, which is slightly bitter, is much better for you.

1 quart dandelion greens
4 slices bacon
¾ cup sour cream
2 teaspoons sugar
2 teaspoons vinegar
2 teaspoons flour
Salt and pepper
2 hard-boiled eggs

Keep the dandelion crisp. Pick it over and wash it, then drain it. Cut the bacon into bits and fry it till crisp. Remove from the pan and drain. Pour all the bacon drippings from the pan but 2 tablespoons; then add a well-blended mixture of the sour cream, sugar, vinegar, flour, salt and pepper. Stir over very low heat till it thickens slightly. Don't let it boil. Just before you are ready to eat, and while the dressing is warm, pour it over the dandelion greens and mix well. The greens should be well coated — you might need more cream. Add the bacon bits and the sliced eggs. Serve immediately with baked or mashed potatoes, farmer's pork sausage, fried ham, smoked pork chops — any kind of pork — and as soon as you taste this wonderful salad your sap will start flowing.

ENDIVE SALAD

Curly, crisp, bleached yellow endive with a warm sour-cream dressing and bacon is a wonderful change from the eternal tossed lettuce salad served with a dinner or buffet supper.

1 medium head endive
3 or 4 slices bacon
2 teaspoons sugar
2 teaspoons flour
2 teaspoons vinegar
1 cup sour cream
Salt and pepper
2 hard-boiled eggs

Wash the endive and let it drain; break it into pieces to make eating easier. Cut the bacon into bits and fry until crisp; remove the bits from the drippings and drain. Pour all but 2 tablespoons of fat from the pan. Mix sugar, flour, vinegar, cream, salt, and pepper; stir till blended then pour into the bacon drippings left in the pan. Over very slow heat, stir the mixture till it thickens a bit — don't let it boil. When the sauce has cooled to lukewarm, pour it over the endive and mix it lightly. Garnish it with sliced eggs and bacon bits and serve at once with meat, potatoes, vegetables, or a casserole. It won't last long.

HOT SLAW

Mother called this "Hot Coleslaw." It's simple and wonderful served with mashed potatoes and farmer's sausage, pork chops, or fried ham. If you live alone, it could be a whole meal.

> **3 or 4 tablespoons butter**
> **4 to 5 cups finely shredded cabbage**
> **1 teaspoon salt**
> **Plenty of pepper**
> **½ cup sour cream**
> **1½ teaspoons vinegar**

In a heavy pan, melt the butter, add the cabbage, salt, and pepper; stir the cabbage over low heat, or simply cover the heavy pan, until it is softened and hot, but not really cooked — certainly not soft and mushy — the spines should remain almost crisp. Blend the sour cream and vinegar and pour over the cabbage, stirring till well coated. Remove from the stove and serve.

DAMPFEKRAUT

Another old-timer — and very good tasting, Bevvy says.

> **4 tablespoons butter, or lard, or bacon fat**
> **8 cups finely sliced cabbage**
> **2 tablespoons vinegar**
> **2 tablespoons flour**
> **1 teaspoon dry mustard**
> **1 teaspoon salt**
> **Pepper**
> **1 egg, well beaten**
> **3 cups milk**
> **2 cups grated cheese**

Melt the butter in a saucepan, pour in the cabbage and cook slightly, stirring constantly to coat it with the butter. Add the vinegar. In another saucepan or double boiler, mix the flour, mustard, salt, and pepper, add the egg blended with the milk; cook till thick. Sprinkle the cabbage with the grated cheese and pour the hot sauce over it. Serve hot.

RED CABBAGE AND APPLE SALAD

This unusual salad looks pretty on a plate and has a pleasant taste. It's wonderful with pork in any form.

3 tablespoons butter
4 cups shredded red cabbage
1 cup thinly sliced apples
2 tablespoons vinegar
2 tablespoons brown sugar
½ teaspoon mustard
1 teaspoon salt
Pepper
½ cup sour cream

Melt the butter in a saucepan, add the cabbage and apple and stir until the butter coats the mixture and there are signs of softening, but the mixture is not really cooked. Add the vinegar, sugar, mustard, and seasonings; simmer another 2 minutes then stir in the sour cream. Serve hot.

WARM POTATO SALAD

If you have ever tasted the warm, creamy, butter-yellow potato salad made in Waterloo County, you'll never again be satisfied with the stiff, white blobs they call potato salad everywhere else.

6 medium potatoes
1 medium onion or fresh chives
Salt
¼ cup butter
1 cup sour cream
2 eggs, beaten
1 tablespoon vinegar
1 tablespoon sugar
Salt and pepper
2 hard-boiled eggs
Parsley or chives

Boil the potatoes in their jackets. Slice the onion finely and sprinkle it with salt, being sure all the onion is salted. In a double boiler or heavy saucepan, melt the butter and stir in the sour cream, eggs, vinegar, sugar, and seasonings; cook long enough to make a sauce that is thick but not stiff. Taste it. If you used large potatoes you might need more cream. Don't be afraid to be lavish: my mother always put in extra butter; my Aunt Rickie, who made the best potato salad I've ever tasted, used the yolks of 6 eggs instead of 2 whole eggs so her salad would look yellower.

Keep the sauce warm or reheat it over hot, but not boiling, water while you peel the hot boiled potatoes and slice them finely. Squeeze the onion slices between your fingers and add them to the dressing — in summer it's prettier to use finely snipped chives. Pour the dressing over the potato slices — still warm — and mix them gently so they won't be mushy. (My mother, when she was making potato salad for a picnic or company, used small round potatoes so all her slices would be the same size.) Put the salad into your prettiest bowl, slice the hard-boiled eggs and decorate the top of the potatoes with them and parsley or chives. Serve warm with cold meats and lettuce and tomatoes.

If you prefer, you might fry four slices of bacon cut into bits, pouring off all the fat but ¼ cupful to be used instead of the butter in the dressing — the bacon bits to be used in the garnishing.

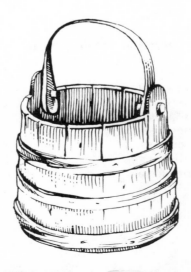

Accompanying Salads

Much of my eating and cooking depends on what in my fridge or freezer needs to be used before it's too late. What do I do with a lemon? What do I do with a green pepper or some limping lettuce?

I have hundreds of cookbooks, and there must be something in some of them. I get out my favourites, including my own Food That Really Schmecks, More Food That Really Schmecks, *and* Schmecks Appeal. *I look in the index and sometimes I find exactly what I am looking for. But other times I have to keep looking, or I get side-tracked and read recipes that sound pretty good and I write, "Try," in the margin beside them. But in the meantime, the lemon or pepper or limp lettuce are waiting, and maybe an hour has passed while I have been pleasantly reading and thinking how good something sounds — like a chocolate soufflé, or a crab bisque, or a nice roast of beef.*

BROCCOLI SALAD

My sister Ruby sent me this recipe; she wrote: "You should like this. I've served it often and everyone wants to know how I did it. You can easily cut it down for two."

  ⅓ **cup mayonnaise**
  3 **tablespoons vinegar**
  2 **tablespoons sugar**
  4 **cups broccoli pieces**
    (peel and cut stems to use as well)
  ½ **cup golden raisins**
  8 **slices bacon, fried crisp and crumbled**

Blend mayonnaise, vinegar, and sugar; add broccoli, raisins, and half the bacon bits. Toss well. Sprinkle with remaining bacon bits and serve.

MIXED COOKED VEGETABLE SALAD

This colourful salad keeps a long time, can be frozen, and may be served as a relish as well as a salad. Margaret Phelan sent me the recipe from her winter home in Arizona, where she served it with a big roast beef dinner.

>   **2 cups cooked beans — or 1 can cut green beans**
>   **2 cups cooked peas — or 1 can small peas**
>   **2 cups cooked corn — or 1 can Mexicana corn**
>   **1 sweet red pepper, diced**
>   **1 green pepper, diced (canned or fresh)**
>   **4 stalks celery, cut fine**
>   **1 medium onion, cut fine**

Drain the cooked vegetables and mix with the pepper, celery, and onion.

>   *Dressing:*
>   **½ cup sugar, or a bit more**
>   **1 cup white vinegar or less**
>   **½ cup water**
>   **1 teaspoon flavoured salt**
>   **½ teaspoon black pepper**

Bring dressing ingredients to a boil, cool, then pour over the vegetables, toss lightly and marinate overnight, or longer. Drain off the dressing before you serve the vegetables, but keep it to put back on the vegetables that are left. Very convenient to have in your fridge.

FOR LAZY LONERS

Scrape, scrub, and eat a carrot every day; it's loaded with vitamins and minerals. Eat a stalk of celery with the leaves; it has calcium, sodium, potassium, phosphorus, iron, and vitamins A and C. Eat a banana. For lunch I often slice a banana over lettuce, sprinkle it with salted peanuts and dribbles of salad dressing. An apple done the same way is good with cubes of cheese.

YOU-NAME-IT SALAD

You'll be amazed at what a good salad you can concoct by rummaging in your fridge and combining a few odds and ends. I'm not suggesting that you use all the ingredients at once.

Lettuce
Cabbage, shredded
Celery stems and leaves
Crisp cauliflower
Sliced olives
Cooked corn, peas, or beans
Tomatoes
Chick peas, kidney beans
Cooked or raw asparagus
Green peppers, red peppers
Chives, green onion and tops, onion slices
Spinach
Soya nuts or others
Shredded coconut
What else is there?

Chop, not too finely, a combination you think you would like; mix it with mayonnaise or toss it with salad dressing, put it on a lettuce leaf, endive, or watercress salad, and you'll have a respectable, attractive, nutritious, non-fattening meal. There are so many variations that you could have fun trying something different every day.

MISS SNIDER'S SALAD

Sarah Snider, a one-time Mennonite and superb cook, used to help when Mother had a party.

Celery, apples, grapes, walnuts, and well-drained **canned pineapple;** cut up as much as you think you need for the occasion. Mix generously with **Mother's Salad Dressing** (page 76) and pile lightly in a lettuce-lined bowl.

FRUIT SALAD

This one was for Mother's bridge club.

Oranges, **grapefruits** and raw or canned **pineapple**, **seedless green grapes** — as much as you need, cut in pieces. Mix with **Mother's Salad Dressing** (page 76).

DILL PICKLE SALAD

This was a company salad that Mother thought was wonderful.

> **3 large dill pickles ("sometimes I use only 2,"
> Mother wrote in her book), cut up
> 3 hard-boiled eggs, cut not too fine
> 3 sweet red peppers, sliced
> 1 little onion, finely sliced
> 2 tablespoons ketchup
> Mother's Salad Dressing (page 76)**

Mix pickles, eggs, peppers, and onion. Combine ketchup and salad dressing, pour over salad. Serve from a bowl.

A TIP

Before you serve guests — or your family — check your fridge to be sure you haven't forgotten something you've slaved over: that special sauce, or the melon balls.

TUNA FISH SPREAD, SALAD, OR DIP

This rich, flavourful concoction can be used various ways and in small amounts.

>8 ounces cream cheese
>1 small can flaked tuna
>2 hard-boiled eggs, chopped fine
>¼ cup mayonnaise
>2 tablespoons onion, chopped fine
>2 tablespoons finely chopped celery
>2 tablespoons chopped pickle (optional)
>½ teaspoon seasoned salt
>½ teaspoon Worcestershire sauce
>⅛ teaspoon curry powder, no more
>⅛ teaspoon pepper

Cream the cheese, add the remaining ingredients, and serve on your favourite crackers. Or use a dollop on a salad plate with other salad things. Or use as a dip. A little goes a long way.

MARY LOU'S DAY-BEFORE SALAD

My niece, Mary Lou Cuff, invited our extended family to spend a winter Sunday in the large, pleasant house in Willowdale where she lives with her professor husband and three children. We all wanted the recipe for the delicious salad she had conveniently made the day before our arrival.

>1 head iceberg lettuce
>2 stalks celery, cut up
>1 green pepper, cut up
>1 large onion, finely sliced
>14-ounce can of peas, heated and drained
>⅓ cup mayonnaise
>2 tablespoons grated cheese
>½ cup crisp bacon bits

In a serving bowl, put a layer of bite-size pieces of iceberg lettuce (a whole head if you think you need that much). Over that, put the celery, then the pepper, then the onion, then the peas. Spread the mayonnaise over all and top with cheese and bacon bits.

Winter Salads

Every fall at the farmers' market I buy the biggest, heaviest green cabbage I can find. I wrap it tightly in a plastic bag and put it on the bed in my guest room, which in winter I heat only enough to keep fruits and vegetables from freezing. Then almost every week I fetch my cabbage to the kitchen, carefully pull off a couple of leaves, and slice or chop them to make a salad for me alone — or a few more leaves for visitors. I wrap up my cabbage again, put it back on the bed with the onions, apples, oranges, and grapefruit, and I am grateful that it will probably last as long as the snow flies.

In winter I don't drive into town any oftener than I absolutely have to. Sometimes our lane is iced in and I can't go. I only occasionally buy fresh imported vegetables. I do try to keep lettuce, celery, and carrots in the bottom drawer of my fridge, so I can concoct a salad whenever I want one. I keep tins of vegetables in my cupboard and frozen ones in my freezer. And always there is my cabbage, which can be used in so many ways: in hot slaw, with cranberries, pineapple, or beets, or marinated and crisp to be eaten with meat and potatoes.

CRANBERRY-CABBAGE SALAD

A colourful, crisp, tart salad that goes well with chicken, turkey, or pork.

> **6 cups finely shredded red cabbage**
> **1 cup cooked, drained cranberries**
> **1 cup sliced celery**
> **Sour cream with Mother's Salad Dressing (page 76)**

Mix all the ingredients just before serving.

CABBAGE-PINEAPPLE SALAD

This is my mother's favourite company salad — with ham, chicken, cold cuts, or roast pork.

1 small head cabbage
20 marshmallows, each cut into 4 pieces (or less)
½ cup milk
1 cup cut-up celery
1 cup drained pineapple chunks, cut in half
1 cup Mother's Salad Dressing (page 76) made by
    mixing 3 tablespoons basic dressing with 1 cup
    whipped cream

Slice or shred the cabbage about ⅛ inch wide. (You should have about 6 cups.) Soak marshmallows in the milk for about 15 minutes. Mix the cabbage, celery, marshmallows, and pineapple and stir in the dressing so all the ingredients are generously covered. Mother serves hers in a hand-painted bowl with bits of parsley and red pepper to pretty it.

MARINATED CABBAGE

If you don't always have fresh greens to make a salad in winter, it's great to have something like this to put on the table instead.

4 cups finely shredded red or white cabbage
1 large onion, sliced thin
¼ cup sugar
½ teaspoon salt
¼ cup vinegar
½ teaspoon dry mustard
2 tablespoons sugar
1½ teaspoons celery seed
¼ cup salad oil

Put the cabbage, onion, sugar, and salt in a bowl. Bring the vinegar, mustard, and sugar to a boil. Add the celery seed and the oil. Pour hot over the cabbage and chill overnight. Drain before serving. Return to jar what isn't used — it will keep for a couple of weeks in your fridge.

BEET AND RED-CABBAGE SALAD

This is something I never want to be without. It is so useful to bring out to serve in the winter with a dinner that needs a bit of colour or zest. While you're making it, you might as well fill several jars and put them away in a cool place where it will keep for a year. Mother gave us this every time we went to her house for dinner.

> **3 or 4 quarts beets**
> **1 small head red cabbage**
> **2 or 3 teaspoons grated horseradish (optional)**
> **1 cup water**
> **2 cups white vinegar**
> **½ cup sugar**
> **1 tablespoon salt**
> **¼ teaspoon pepper**

Boil the beets till tender. Drain and cover the beets with cold water. Slip off their skins. Chop the beets — not fine enough to be mushy but not in big lumps. Shred or slice the cabbage fairly thin, then add to beets. Add the horseradish. In a small saucepan, bring the water to a boil. Stir in vinegar, sugar, and salt; then add pepper and stir. Pour this hot solution over the beet mixture, then stir together. Spoon the salad into sterilized jars, making sure the liquid covers the beets and cabbage. If you haven't enough, you can easily mix up a bit more. To serve, drain off the liquid. Whatever isn't used can be put back into the jar and kept for the next time you want a ready-made sour. Mother served this with almost every company dinner. It goes well with a roast — or anything.

CRISP AND SLIMMING COLESLAW

This is a breeze if you have a food processer. It fills the gap when you need a salad in winter and haven't enough lettuce to toss. It will stay tangy and tasty for days in your fridge or a cold room.

⅓ cup sugar
3 tablespoons cider vinegar
3 tablespoons lemon juice
½ teaspoon garlic salt
¼ teaspoon celery seed
3 cups chopped cabbage
3 carrots, chopped
1 medium onion, finely chopped
  (or sliced green onions)
1 stalk celery, chopped
¼ cup chopped green pepper — if you have it

Combine the first five ingredients in a serving bowl. Add the chopped vegetables and toss lightly. Cover and refrigerate for at least four hours. You'll be amazed how many people will want second helpings.

Oil and Vinegar Salads

*I asked Nancy and her friend Miriam from Chicago to give
me some ideas for salads. Nancy said, "We always have the
same thing: lettuce or spinach leaves, onion, garlic,
tomatoes, bean or alfalfa sprouts if we can get them, with
an oil and vinegar dressing. That's it."*

*"Yes, for me too; it's always the same," Miriam told me.
"Every day the same."*

*Though there is the possibility of infinite variety in
salads, many people have the same one every day. So do
many restaurants, with dressings limited to oil and
vinegar, or Miracle Whip, the dominant taste being vinegar.*

*I'd say, "How boring." But many people won't try
anything else.*

TOMATO SALAD WITH HERBS

2 pounds tomatoes
1 tablespoon sugar
1 cup finely chopped parsley
1 cup chopped fresh basil leaves
    (or 2 tablespoons dried basil)
1 teaspoon salt
½ teaspoon dry mustard
¼ cup olive oil
1 tablespoon or less wine vinegar
Freshly ground black pepper

Slice medium or large tomatoes — keep small ones whole. Arrange in a salad bowl, sprinkle with sugar, parsley, and basil.
Blend the salt, mustard, olive oil, vinegar, and pepper, then
pour over the tomatoes. Marinate 2 hours before serving.

RALPH'S GREEK SALAD

Ever since my brother-in-law visited Greece, he has been treating people to his own variation of a Greek salad. He says it's all you need for a meal, with a fat, hot bun.

> 1 Spanish, Italian, or any mild onion,
>   finely sliced in rings
> 2 tomatoes, cut in wedges
> 1 cup crumbled feta cheese, or any other kind if
>   you don't have feta
> ½ green pepper, sliced and cut in thin rings
>   or squares, not too fine
> Parsley, a few sprigs, not finely cut
> 2 or 3 inches cucumber, sliced thin
> ¼ cup ripe olives, cut in quarters

Combine everything in a bowl. The Greeks Ralph visited didn't use lettuce, but Ralph tears and tosses some in. He makes the dressing as close to serving time as possible:

> *Dressing:*
> 1 clove garlic, mashed
> 1 tablespoon wine vinegar
> 7 tablespoons olive oil, but another oil will do
> Salt and pepper

Mash the garlic clove and add it to the vinegar. (Use lemon juice if you don't have a mild vinegar.) Add 4 tablespoons oil and beat with a fork, add salt and pepper, then 3 more tablespoons oil. Blend very well before drizzling it over the salad greens, mixing it lightly.

Ralph likes this so well that he often serves it as an accompaniment to a dinner or buffet supper.

POT LUCK BEAN SALAD

This bean salad appears at every pot luck supper I've ever attended. I'm not fond of it, but many people must be because it seems to disappear every time. It's easy to make ahead of time and uses ingredients you no doubt have in your cupboard.

> **1 medium can cut wax beans
>   (or 1 package frozen, cooked)
> 1 can cut green beans
>   (or 1 package frozen, cooked)
> 1 can red kidney beans
> 1 can green lima beans
>   (or 1 package frozen, cooked)**

Combine beans in a bowl.

> *Dressing:*
> **½ cup red wine or cider vinegar
> ½ cup salad oil
> ½ cup sugar
> 1 teaspoon salt
> Pinch of pepper
> 1 large onion (Spanish preferred),
>   cut in chunks or sliced
> 1 green pepper, cut in pieces (optional)
> ½ teaspoon basil
> 1 tablespoon cut-up parsley**

Combine dressing ingredients and pour over beans. Chill overnight. Before serving, drain. Keep the marinade for whatever beans are left over. It will keep for quite a while in your fridge.

This should serve 16 to 20 people — especially if they don't like it any better than I do.

WATERCRESS SALAD

You can prepare this a few hours ahead, and as long as you don't add the dressing until the last minute, it will be crisp to the end.

5 or 6 cups watercress
Lettuce leaves — as many as you think you'll need
1 clove garlic, cut in half
4 tablespoons olive oil
1½ tablespoons vermouth
Salt
Freshly ground pepper
A pinch of sugar
1½ teaspoons lemon juice

Wash, dry, and break the watercress into neat sprigs. Wash and dry the lettuce leaves. Tear into bite-sized pieces. Rub salad bowl with cut garlic. Add watercress and lettuce. Combine oil and vermouth with salt, pepper, sugar, and lemon juice in a screw-top jar. Shake well until blended. Pour over greens and mix thoroughly with your hands until each leaf is glistening. Serve immediately.

Main Dish Salads

For me, many salads can be a complete meal — perhaps with home-baked bread or hot biscuits.

One day I watched Nancy toss a salad of mixed greens that I thought was enough for four people. But she sat down and ate every bit of it herself.

Nancy has a lithe, beautiful figure.

SALAD WITH PASTA

With a little ingenuity you can put together a great salad, heap it up in a beautiful bowl, and feed a dozen people.

> **4 cups cooked macaroni or any fancy pasta**
> **2 to 4 cups cubes of cooked chicken, turkey, ham,**
>   **or flaked tuna, salmon, or shrimps,**
>   **or whatever you think would be good**
> **1 cup thinly sliced celery**
> **1 cup seedless green grapes, or ½ cup sliced**
>   **green stuffed olives (optional)**
> **½ to 1 cup slivered toasted almonds,**
>   **pecans, or walnuts**
> **5 or 6 hard-boiled eggs, quartered and sliced**

Put whatever you decide to use into a mixing bowl. In a blender or food processor, blend the following:

> *Dressing:*
> **1¼ cups mayonnaise**
> **¼ cup white wine**
> **5 or 6 sprigs parsley**
> **1 sweet red or green pepper**

Pour the dressing over the salad, mix well, and chill until you are ready to serve it. You might need more mayonnaise and some salt. Keep tasting as you put this together. It's worth it. Line your beautiful bowl with crisp lettuce leaves, pour in the salad, and let your guests have their fling.

BE PREPARED

Always keep small tins of ham, chicken, turkey, tuna, salmon, and shrimp on your pantry shelf to be used in salads or quiches. (When you see them on special at the supermarket, you might buy several cans.)

FROZEN RICE OR PASTA

Often when I'm making a rice or pasta dish I'll cook more rice or pasta than I need, drain it well, put it into a plastic container and freeze it for future use. It comes in handy so often when I need only a cupful or two in a salad — or whatever.

RICE AND CHICKEN SALAD

Just as good made with ham, turkey, tuna, salmon, shrimp, or what-have-you.

> 1 to 2 cups cooked, diced chicken,
>   leftover, frozen, or a small tin
> 1 to 2 cups cooked rice
> 1 cup green peas, raw, frozen, or cooked
> 1 long stalk celery, sliced
> ½ green pepper, diced (optional)
> 2 tablespoons chopped parsley
> 1 tablespoon minced onion,
>   or finely chopped chives, or green onion
> 1 tablespoon or more chutney or relish
> ½ to 1 cup mayonnaise
> 2 tablespoons sour cream
> A few slices of stuffed olives (optional)

Mix all the ingredients but the chutney, mayonnaise, and sour cream. Keep the mixture in your fridge and add the chutney blended with the mayonnaise and sour cream just before serving on fresh lettuce or a ring of watercress with a garnish of radish, tomato, or olives. A few toasted almonds are a pleasant addition as well.

GORDON WAGNER'S SALMON SALAD

When Gordon read my story of the Cookie War in *Saturday Night* magazine, he called me from his home on Comox Bay, Vancouver Island. He said he was flying east soon to find some ancestors and he'd like to come to see me. He stayed with a nephew in Brampton but came every day to Waterloo Region, where he called on Breithaupts and Staeblers, Knechtels and Devitts, whose names were among the fifteen hundred listed in his genealogy.

Because he writes poems and short pieces about people and was working on a book about his great-grandmother Breithaupt, I introduced him to Hannah and Eva, who enjoyed his stories as much as I did. With each of us he left a tin of B.C. spring salmon, which had been canned as soon as it was brought in on a boat.

One day when he came to my house he said he wanted to make his secret salmon salad for our lunch. Here is his secret:

> **1 tin salmon, drained (but keep the liquid)**
> **A few lettuce leaves, cut in ½-inch slices**
> **1 long stalk celery, cut fine**
> **6 spears asparagus (optional, in season)**
> **¼ medium onion, chopped fine**
> **¼ cup mayonnaise**
> **1 teaspoon sugar**
> **1 tablespoon ketchup**
> **1 teaspoon juice from a jar of sweet pickles**
> **— or lemon juice**
> **1 hard-boiled egg**

Gordon minced the salmon and mixed it with the vegetables, then made the dressing. To the salmon liquid he added the mayonnaise, sugar, ketchup, and juice. He said he likes his salad to be a bit sloppy.

Gordon poured the dressing over the salad ingredients and gave it a good stir, scraped all of it into one of my Quimper bowls, sliced a hard-boiled egg over the top, and with my fresh home-baked bread we ate all but one small serving, which I finished up that same evening. Gordon said one tin usually makes enough salad for four.

CRAB MEAT SALAD

I think this is my absolute favourite salad. One time Harold
Horwood brought a pound of frozen **crab meat** to my house.
After it thawed, he sprinkled over it the **juice of half a lemon**,
then mixed it with finely sliced **celery** and as much **mayonnaise** as was needed to hold it together. On lettuce leaves and
with fresh homemade bread, we ate every bit.

CRAB NUGGET SALAD

Allen Detweiler comes to my house with a truck full of tempting
frozen seafoods, steaks, chicken breasts, fresh and salt-water
fish, and ¾-inch cubes of crab nuggets, which are really fish
blended with crab and attractively tinted the colour of crab. I
always buy boxes of sole, steaks, and crab to keep in my freezer
for whenever I want them.

The **crab nuggets** are wonderful to have for a quickly made
salad tossed with **finely sliced celery** and **mayonnaise** on
lettuce leaves. People who come here think it's a great treat, and
I often have it when I want to treat myself.

SALMON OR TUNA AND RICE SALAD

This salad could be a complete meal on a hot summer day.

¼ **cup blanched almonds**
2 **tablespoons vegetable oil**
1 **tin tuna or salmon**
4 **cups cold cooked rice**
1 **cup whole-kernel corn — or slightly more**
1 **small green pepper, seeded and chopped**
2 **tablespoons sliced green onion or chives**
12 **stuffed olives — if you have them**
    — cut in halves
Salt and pepper

Cut the almonds in quarters and gently cook in the oil until
golden. Remove the almonds from the oil and mix them with the
other ingredients. Chill before serving with dressing you can
pass around.

APPLE SALAD FOR HILDA

When Hilda came to clean my house, every morning for almost twenty years, she wanted an apple salad for lunch. And I gave it to her. It's refreshing and doesn't take long to make on a busy day.

> **2 or 3 large apples**
> **1 thick stalk celery**
> **Handful of walnuts**
> **½ cup sliced cabbage (optional)**
> **¼ cup cubed cheddar (optional)**
> **¼ cup raisins (optional)**
> **Enough mayonnaise to coat everything**

Core and slice the apples, chop the celery and nuts. Mix with any optional ingredients and mayonnaise. Serve on lettuce. Mother's Salad Dressing (page 76) blended with sour cream is good with this.

JELLIED APPLE SALAD

If you want the same salad prepared ahead of time and for more people, you might add ¼ cup lemon juice to **a package of lime or lemon jelly powder**, dissolved and chilled to the consistency of raw egg whites. Stir in the rest of the ingredients, turn into a mold and chill until it is firm. Serve with lettuce and mayonnaise and fresh, hot cheese biscuits.

Jellied Salads

*I can't imagine anyone making a jellied or molded salad
for anything but a party. Like jewels in a crown, they look
quite impressive, and guests always say, "How pretty. I
hate to cut into it." But served with hot things on a plate,
they melt and wet. I seldom make jellied salads, I can't
bear the suspense of knowing if they'll come out of the mold
all in one piece; if they have substance, the hazard is
greater; if they are merely jellied liquid, I'd rather drink
liquid. I'll give you a few recipes that I've enjoyed at the
homes of friends who are braver than I. Good luck to you.*

LADIES' PARTY CHEESE RING

They'll say, "Ooh" and "Aah" when they taste this, and they'll
all want the recipe. Tell them to buy my book.

> 1 tablespoon plain gelatine
> ½ cup dry white wine, heated
> 1 cup crumbled Roquefort or blue cheese
> ½ cup mayonnaise
> 3 ounces cream cheese
> A thin slice of mild onion
> 2 tablespoons lemon juice
> ½ teaspoon Worcestershire sauce
> Salt and celery salt
> 1 cup whipping cream
> Fresh fruit
> Super French Dressing (page 78)

Dissolve the gelatin in the heated wine in your blender, then add
and blend all the other ingredients but the cream. Whip the
cream in a bowl and fold it into the blended mixture. Turn it all
into an oiled ring mold. Chill until firm. Unmold on crisp salad
greens and fill the centre with fresh fruit. Make it look really
pretty with grapes, melon balls, slices of peach, apple, or what-
have-you. Beside it on the table have a dish of French dressing.

FISH MOUSSE AT RUNDLES

This delicacy should not be missed. It was served with crisp cucumber salad and soda bread before the main course. The fish used was leftover salmon.

1 pound flaked cooked fish
1 cup milk
1 slice onion
1 bay leaf
6 peppercorns
2 tablespoons butter
1 teaspoon paprika
3 tablespoons flour
1 teaspoon gelatine
3 tablespoons heavy cream
1 egg white

Pass the fish through a blender for a second or mash it with a fork. Heat the milk with onion, bay leaf, and peppercorns, infuse and strain. Melt the butter, add paprika, cook for 1 minute. Remove from the heat and blend in the flour, add the hot milk and cook to the boiling point. Put away for a while to cool in a bowl, not the pan it was cooked in. Mix the cold sauce with the fish a little at a time. Dissolve the gelatine over heat with a little water, add to the fish mixture. Whip the cream lightly; whisk the egg white and fold both gently into the fish mixture. Pour into a large mold or individual ones. The result was firm and tender, not stiff and rubbery.

Perfect.

PERFECTION SALAD

This was Mother's old stand-by.

1 tablespoon plain gelatine
¼ cup cold water
¼ cup sugar
½ teaspoon salt
1 cup boiling water
¼ cup mild vinegar
1 tablespoon lemon juice
1 sweet red pepper, cut in small pieces
1 cup celery, cut up fine
½ cup finely shredded cabbage
Mayonnaise

Soften gelatine in cold water. Add sugar, salt, and boiling water; stir until dissolved. Add vinegar and lemon juice. Cool and, when mixture begins to stiffen, add chopped vegetables. Turn into individual molds, chill until firm; serve on lettuce, with mayonnaise.

RED TOMATO MOLD

For company, too.

4 cups tomato juice
⅓ cup chopped onion
¼ cup chopped celery leaves
2 tablespoons brown sugar
1 teaspoon salt
2 small bay leaves
4 whole cloves
2 tablespoons plain gelatine
3 tablespoons lemon juice

Combine 2 cups of the tomato juice, onion, celery leaves, sugar, salt, bay leaves, and cloves. Simmer uncovered for 5 minutes. Strain. Meanwhile, soften gelatine in 1 cup of remaining cold tomato juice; dissolve in hot tomato mixture. Add lemon juice and remaining cup of tomato juice. Pour into a 5-cup ring mold, or individual molds; chill till firm.

MARY'S PINEAPPLE AND CUCUMBER SALAD WITH WHITE WINE

Beside this in my own hand-written notebook I have written. "Fresh cool taste and easy to do."

>   2 tablespoons gelatine
>   1 cup hot water
>   1 cucumber, sliced
>   1 green pepper, diced
>   1 cup dry white wine or dry sherry
>   ½ cup sugar
>   2 tablespoons lemon juice
>   ¾ teaspoon salt
>   1½ cups crushed pineapple
>   Mayonnaise

Dissolve the gelatine in the hot water in your blender, then add all the other ingredients but the pineapple. Blend until the vegetables are finely cut. Pour into a bowl and chill until mixture begins to thicken, then add the pineapple. Mix well, turn into a mold and chill until firm. Carefully unmold (and good luck to you) on salad greens and serve with mayonnaise in a bowl alongside.

NORA MYER'S JELLIED RHUBARB SALAD

Very pretty and tasty on a cold luncheon plate served in Nora's beautiful old stone house near Cambridge.

>   4 cups rhubarb, cut in 1-inch pieces
>   ½ cup water
>   ¾ cup sugar
>   1 package strawberry jelly powder
>   1 cup cold water
>   1 tablespoon grated orange rind
>   ¼ cup chopped nuts (optional)
>   1 cup finely chopped celery (optional)
>   Cottage cheese

Simmer the rhubarb, water, and sugar until the rhubarb is tender, about 10 minutes. Remove from the heat, sprinkle in the jelly powder and stir till it's dissolved. Stir in the cold water and orange rind (and nuts and celery, if you want your salad to be crisp). Pour the mixture into a ring mold rinsed in cold water. Chill till firm. Turn out on a platter, put salad greens around, and cottage cheese in the centre.

Without the celery you could use it as a dessert with whipped cream and cookies.

CRANBERRY SALAD

Another company one. Pretty and very good, too.

    4 cups cranberries
    Juice of 1 can of pineapple and
        enough hot water to make 3½ cups
    2 tablespoons plain gelatine (or a little more)
    ½ cup cold water
    2 cups sugar
    ½ cup walnuts, chopped
    1 cup grapes, cut in half and seeded
    1 can pineapple, diced
    Mayonnaise

Cook the cranberries in the pineapple juice and hot water. Soak the gelatine in the cold water; add the hot cranberries and the sugar, and stir till sugar is dissolved; cool. When cold, add nuts, grapes, diced pineapple, and stir well. Cool until firm, in individual molds. Turn out and serve with mayonnaise on shredded lettuce.

Salad Dressings — Be Inventive

Many dishes are invented because you don't happen to have the ingredients required for a recipe. Then what? You make whatever it is without them, or you substitute, or you improvise, and if you do that, you'll have something new and different, maybe wonderful, maybe yucky. Give it a French name and your eaters will be impressed — one way or another.

If you wait till you get all the ingredients to make a new recipe — as you should do to be fair and successful — you might never achieve it. My friend Kath told me she had read a good-sounding recipe that used cardomom seeds, of which she had none. By the time she had finally bought some a year later, she had forgotten where she saw the recipe that needed them.

MOTHER'S SALAD DRESSING

A little of this thick, nippy dressing goes a long way and seems to be just right with any salads that have fruit in them — or cabbage, or almost anything.

> **1 teaspoon flour**
> **1 teaspoon dry mustard**
> **Pinch of salt**
> **½ cup water**
> **1 egg, well beaten**
> **¼ cup brown sugar**
> **¼ cup vinegar**
> **Sprinkle of cayenne pepper**
> **Whipped or sour cream**

Mix the flour, mustard, and salt with the water, add to the beaten egg and brown sugar. Slowly stir in the vinegar and sprinkle in the cayenne. Thicken the mixture in a double boiler, over hot water, stirring all the time. Chill this basic dressing before you blend a little of it with the whipped or sour cream. How much cream you use depends on the size of your salad and how nippy you like your dressing. Taste it. The basic dressing keeps well for ages in your fridge, tightly covered. Also, if it's mixed with sour cream it will keep as long as the sour cream would without it.

BASIC DRESSING

This oil and vinegar dressing can be made more interesting and more palatable if you vary it to suit whatever salad you're making.

> **1 cup salad oil — of your choice**
> **½ cup vinegar — of your choice**
> **1 teaspoon salt**
> **Pinch of pepper**
> **2 teaspoons sugar or honey**
> **½ teaspoon paprika**
> **½ teaspoon dry mustard (optional**

Put all the ingredients into a jar or blender and shake or blend until well mixed. Cover and keep in fridge. Mix well before using.

MINT DRESSING

Especially good with fruit salads. Strip **five sprigs of mint** of their leaves and blend with your Basic Dressing until they are very, very finely chopped.

CHILI OR CHUTNEY DRESSING

Add **3 or 4 tablespoons of chili sauce** or **chutney** to the Basic Dressing and blend fairly well. It is fine with meat, fish, or seafood salads — or simply with greens.

GINGER DRESSING

Good with fruit salads: To 1 cup of Basic Dressing add **1 tablespoon preserved ginger** with syrup. Blend well.

CHEESE DRESSING

With the Basic Dressing, blend until perfectly smooth — or leave lumpy — ¾ cup cheese — Danish, Gorgonzola, Roquefort, Stilton, or whatever — the stronger the better.

NUTS IN DRESSING

This adds a piquant touch to any salad but especially mixed greens. Sauté ½ **cup** (or less) **chopped or whole almonds, pecans, sunflower seeds**, or **walnuts** in a little **butter** until lightly browned — or toast them in your oven. Blend with the Basic Dressing for just a second.

SUPER FRENCH DRESSING

To Basic Dressing add:

¾ cup ketchup
1 small onion, quartered
½ teaspoon celery seed

Blend until perfectly smooth.

CURRY DRESSING

This adds a bit of mystery to salads with meats, vegetables, seafood, or chicken.
   To the Basic Dressing simply add:

1 teaspoon curry powder
A sliver of garlic (optional)
A few sprigs of parsley
A slice of onion

Blend until smooth. You could add 2 or 3 tablespoons of chili sauce or chutney or ketchup to give this more colour and flavour. But suit yourself.

These are only a few suggestions. You can try any number of flavours that will make your salads more exciting. Don't be afraid to experiment. That's how great recipes are born.

POPPY-SEED FRUIT-SALAD DRESSING

Helen Dier loved to cook. She got this recipe when she was visiting in Dallas, but she wasn't in the TV series.

1½ cups sugar
⅔ cup vinegar
2 teaspoons dry mustard
2 teaspoons salt
3 tablespoons onion juice
2 cups salad oil
2 tablespoons poppy seeds

Stir together sugar, vinegar, mustard, and salt. Add onion juice and blend thoroughly. Add oil slowly, beating until mixture becomes thick. Then add poppy seeds and chill. Serve cold over cabbage, avocado, or fresh fruit salads.

TOSSED SALAD DRESSING

Phil Kitchen's Wellesley Township neighbours taught her how to keep a tossed salad crisp a long time before serving.

½ cup vinegar
½ cup water
3 tablespoons sugar
1 tablespoon salad oil
Seasonings

Blend the vinegar, water, and sugar, then toss lightly with the salad greens and keep in a cool place, for several hours if necessary. Just before serving drain off the liquid, add to it the oil and seasonings, and toss it again with your greens.

HAROLD'S NUTRITIOUS SALAD DRESSING

When Harold Horwood was writer-in-residence at the University of Waterloo, he lived in a house with students. Every week he made two or three batches of salad dressing. "I can't seem to give them enough of it," he told me. "They use it as a dip with vegetables and on salads. If I don't stop them they'll eat it by the spoonful." Harold says engivita yeast, which can be purchased at health-food stores, is as nutritious as brewer's yeast but has a pleasant nutty flavour.

> **2 eggs**
> **1 teaspoon salt**
> **1 teaspoon dry mustard**
> **1 teaspoon honey**
> **2 tablespoons cider vinegar**
> **1 tablespoon lemon juice**
> **2 tablespoons engivita yeast**
> **3 tablespoons dry parsley flakes**
> **1 cup vegetable oil**

In a blender, place eggs, salt, mustard, and honey. Blend. Add vinegar and lemon juice. Turn on blender and give it a whirl. Add yeast and blend again. Add parsley. Blend. Then add oil very, very slowly while blending until the desired thickness is reached. Refrigerate — it will stay fresh for a long time if you're not greedy.

SEAFOOD DRESSING

This is also good with vegetable salads and avocado.

½ cup tomato sauce
½ cup mayonnaise
½ cup cream

Blend ingredients and chill.

DRESSING FOR WARM POTATO SALAD

Warm, creamy, butter-yellow, there is none better than this. I wish I could convert the world to it so I'd never again be confronted by those stiff, white blobs served up with an ice cream scoop.

¼ cup butter
1 cup sour cream
2 eggs, beaten
1 tablespoon vinegar
1 tablespoon sugar
Salt and pepper

Melt the butter and stir the sour cream, eggs, vinegar, sugar, and seasonings into it; cook long enough in a double boiler or heavy saucepan to make a sauce that is thick but not stiff. Taste it. Pour it over and mix it with 5 or 6 medium-sized, warm, sliced potatoes and onion or chives to be garnished with hard-cooked eggs. Don't be afraid to be lavish; you might need more cream.

You can prepare this before you need it and reheat it prior to serving.

EVA'S MOM'S MAYONNAISE

Rich, creamy, and popular long before Mr. Kraft flooded the world with Miracle Whip.

> 1 cup water
> ½ cup vinegar
> 1 cup white sugar
> 2 tablespoons flour
> 1 tablespoon dry mustard
> ¾ teaspoon salt
> 2 eggs
> 1 cup whole milk

Heat the water and vinegar. Blend the sugar, flour, mustard, and salt together to prevent lumping. Beat the eggs somewhat and blend with the milk, then stir into the dry ingredients carefully, then into the hot water and vinegar. You don't need to do it in a double boiler if you keep stirring it over low heat. Keep stirring until it thickens; it won't take long. Let cool and it will keep in your fridge for a long time.

FROZEN CHIVES AND PARSLEY

In the spring when the chives in your garden are flourishing, cut them and arrange them in bundles, wrap them tightly in plastic bags and freeze them to provide fresh greens through the winter. Simply hold the bundle and slice off whatever you need. Do the same with parsley.

CHIVE CHEESE DRESSING, SPREAD, OR DIP

This is one of my favourite things; I often make a meal of it spread generously on my own biscuits or crackers. Sometimes I use it as a salad dressing over chopped mixed vegetables. Or as a dip. Kath invented it because she doesn't like the texture of cottage cheese.

> **A good handful of chives, cut in ¼-inch pieces**
> **Creamed cottage cheese**
> **Salt and pepper**

Put the chives in your blender or food processer and gradually add the cheese as you keep blending, until the whole thing is a lovely soft green and smooth as sour cream. If you have dry cottage cheese, you could add sour cream or yogurt to give it the moisture it needs. I'm not fooling: this is terrific! And easy.

HERB CHEESE OR PARSLEY CHEESE

The same as chive cheese but use **herbs** or **parsley** instead of chives. Or try a combination.

SOUR CREAM

You can make your own sour cream from whipping cream by stirring in a tablespoon of buttermilk and leaving it at room temperature till it thickens.

MOTHER-IN-LAW'S SALAD DRESSING

Have you ever noticed how many men want the kind of salad dressing their mothers used to make? You might as well humour them — it's easy to make this.

> ½ cup (or less) vinegar
> ½ cup water
> ⅓ cup sugar
> 2 heaping tablespoons flour
> 1 teaspoon dry mustard
> 1 teaspoon salt
> 1 egg, beaten

Put everything but the egg into a double boiler, mix well and cook until the mixture is very thick. While hot pour it over the beaten egg in a bowl and beat again. To make sure the egg is cooked, I pour the whole bit back into the double boiler and stir it for 2 minutes. It keeps well in the fridge and middle-aged men, especially, think it is wonderful.

INDEX